For the Love of
My Country

For the Love of My Country

Desert Storm

Blessed are the peacemakers.

—Matt 5:9

BARBARA J. EVANS

To order additional copies of this book, contact:
Xlibris Corporation
1-888-795-4274
www.Xlibris.com
Orders@Xlibris.com
15417

Contents

Dedication

I'd like to thank my husband, Kenneth, for his patience and understanding of the many hours it took in writing and publishing this book. I'd also like to thank my sons Don and Wayne Evans, my mother Lucille Amos, my siblings, especially my sister Carol Giorsetti and her husband John for taking care of everything so I didn't have to worry. This book is also dedicated to the military, their family members, and civilians attached to the military in a deployed status; and more importantly to the American Red Cross volunteers and paid staff. God bless all of you.

PROLOGUE

It was February 15, 1991 at 0200 hrs (2:00 a.m. civilian time) in Saudi Arabia. I was with the G-1 Forward Command group located at Log Base Echo approximately 15-30 miles from the Iraqi border. We were all impatiently waiting for the air war to end so we could start "G Day", the ground war.

I was sitting on a small desolate sand dune watching the world's greatest tanks, Abrams and Bradleys, quietly and slowly drift by undetected by those sleeping. They were headed for last minute preparations in Camp Garcia about 25 kms West of us before they crossed the Iraq border to begin the "Mother of all Wars." I wondered how these tanks could be so quiet. I remembered as a small child watching WWII movies. The tanks were always noisy and obnoxious and seemed as if you could hear them coming from far off . . . but not these tanks. These quiet, but bodacious tanks were Abrams and Bradleys, the worlds best, and they were ready for action. Half of the world was asleep but not our American forces for they were working round-the-clock and were moving closer to their target. Iraq. War. These soldiers were Iron soldiers, 1AD (1st Armored Division) of the US ARMY, 7th Corp. from Germany.

As I watched each of them drive by I couldn't help but feel an ice-cold wind blow across my cheeks bringing with it what seemed to be thousands of sand particles. My dishwater blonde, fine, short hair was being blown from a northern direction and I could feel the baby powder type sand find its way all over my body. It didn't matter how many layers of clothing you had on, the sand still found a way to penetrate through anything and cling to everything. As I watched each of these tanks slowly go by with gallant soldiers who were putting their life on the line for freedom, liberty, and oil, tears began to swell in my eyes as I wondered how many of these young men and women were going to die. How many will leave families behind? Will thousands die as predicted by the news media and our military? I couldn't help but think about many of them being the ages of my two sons, 19 and 21 years of age.

I stared into the pitch-black sky and noticed how it was a darker black than I had ever seen in my entire life. The coal black nights were always surrounded with thousands of beautiful stars. There was always this one bright star, which outshone all of them. I had been told that it was the Star of David, and it seemed to be watching over us, Israel, and all of the Arab countries. I didn't know how true it was, but I didn't really care, it just sounded good.

As I looked far ahead into Iraq, I could see arrays of large flashes of lights burst, glow, and then disappear. There was no sound, just total darkness and then quick flashes. I knew that every time I saw this spectacular glow that bombs were being dropped by our American and Allied forces in Iraq, killing the enemy's powerful military force. It was interesting, because we couldn't see the bombs actually being dropped. All we could see were the after affects. Prayerfully this bombing was doing enough damage to Iraq's supplies that we in turn would not lose as many lives as the world's media seemed to think we would. I then wondered how many of those flyboys dropping the bombs were from Davis Monthan Air Force Base, out of Tucson, Arizona, my hometown. My friend, Captain George Marshall was stationed there and flew AWACS (Airborne Warning and Control System). Then, my mind started reflecting back to events leading me here.

It was mid November, 1990, and I met George when I was flying out of Tucson International Airport headed for an interview with the American Red Cross in San Francisco, CA. This was where I had my first interview to determine if I was going to be accepted for training, and deployment to Saudi Arabia.

I had never been on a plane before. George noticed I seemed a bit nervous to him, so he politely came over and introduced himself.

"Hi, I'm George Marshall. Are you from Tucson or are you flying back home to California?"

"Ummm . . . Hi", I said. "Yes, I'm from Tucson, I'm actually headed to California for an interview with the American Red Cross to possibly deploy to the Gulf region. I'm currently working in Tucson for Pima County Human Resources and they're allowing me to take a leave of absence from work to go for this interview. They think I'm crazy for volunteering to go to Desert Shield, but they're supporting me in my decision. It looks like I'm starting off with all kinds of new adventures in my life, with this being my first one. You see, I've never flown before, so this is my first new experience."

George broke out in laughter and said, "I can't believe you've never flown before. Where have you been? We're in the 90's and you haven't flown? Have you been locked up? No wonder you seem nervous! And you volunteered to go to Saudi Arabia? Why? Oh my gosh! This is unreal!" And he continued laughing. Then he said, "I'm going to say goodbye to my folks in California because I'm due to deploy to the Gulf. I'm a Captain in the Air Force. I fly AWACS." Next thing I knew, he proceeded to tell me everything about planes. After his long explanation, he asked me, "So why would a woman like you want to go to a desert filled with soldiers?"

I guess one look at me was kind of shocking. I weighed 118 lbs., my hair was to my shoulders nicely done and my nails were beautifully long and had just been manicured. I was wearing an attractive black professional two-piece business suit with a loosely fitting light-colored pink blouse. My skirt was somewhat short and tight fitting with matching black, 2-inch high heels. I guess I didn't look like someone ready for "war".

I didn't like his comment about my wanting to go to the desert filled with soldiers, but then, he seemed a bit egotistical, and he really didn't know me. The last thing on earth I wanted was a man. My husband had died two years earlier and sadly, I had been plagued by men who couldn't "just be friends". They seemed to always want to get serious, but I wasn't ready for that. My desire to go to War was for the welfare of families and helping in any way I could. I also knew that if they initiated the draft, that one of my sons would probably be drafted. My heart told me that if anyone needed to put their life on the line it would be me because I had nothing at home keeping me from helping my Country. I loved my country. But I knew George wouldn't understand that, and I wasn't about to try to explain it to him. After all, he was a total stranger.

By looking at him, I estimated that he was about five years younger than me, was about five foot, eight inches tall, and had a small build. His personality was very cheerful, yet he would bounce from one subject to another. More specifically, he had mentioned that he was engaged, hoping to marry within the year, that is if he survived the escalation of the Persian Gulf War.

We had a long talk, of which he explained to me about the AWACs he flew and what his mission would be in Iraq. "I have a variety of tasks I'll be responsible for, such as flying AWACS which consist of keeping track of sorties being flown by hundreds of coalition aircraft; surveillance; directing air strikes; interdiction of Iraqi airplanes; and protection of high value aircraft while conducting intelligence and ground surveillance."

He continued talking while my fists were entrenched around the arms of the chair, tightly holding on. I was in first class, by the graciousness of the American Red Cross, but it meant nothing to me. All I knew was that I was above the clouds, as if I were in heaven, and a long way from mother earth, which meant we'd have a long way to fall. But then, I reassured myself that it would be a quick death if the plane went down.

Next thing I knew, we had landed. I knew George had said several things to me as we were flying, but I absorbed very little as I was more concerned about the flight. We then departed quickly and each went our merry way.

I was soon located by Red Cross staff, who escorted me to Western Headquarters where I went through an interview to determine if I would be chosen to go to Desert Shield. There was a panel, and the one woman's name who was asking most of the questions was "Mary". The one question stressed was, "Why do you want to go? It was then followed up with, "Do you realize the danger that you'll be in?"

I opened my heart to them. "I am a single person, having suffered tragedy in my life and I feel I can relate to many of these emergency messages which we'll be dealing with. I've lost my husband and my father. I've had a miscarriage and a full-term stillbirth on Mother's Day a few years ago. None of these were easy. My sons are now grown, and out of my home. If I die, I won't be leaving a child or husband behind, and I'd rather put my life on the line, than someone who has much more to lose. I'm not worried about the danger. I believe in God, and if it's my time to die, then I will die. I love my country and God, and want to help in any way possible. My brother is over there somewhere, and since I've never contributed to our Country, I now have the chance."

After a few more questions, they thanked me for coming and I was soon flying back home.

Upon my return, I went back to work and continued volunteering on my weekends for the Red Cross Chapter in Tucson, working emergency messages for the military.

About two weeks later, I received a phone call from George and he said, "Hi Barbara. Bet you can't guess who this is!"

"No, I don't know who it is," I said.

"It's George. The guy you met on the plane. I'm in the Persian Gulf right now! I thought I'd give you a call and see if you were still going."

"Oh! Well hi there! How on earth did you get my phone number? Why are you calling me? What are you doing there?" (As I laughed surprisingly to myself.) I noticed that he seemed to be in a hurry and was excited.

"I wanted to tell you that me and the rest of my squadron are situated in the proximity of the United Arab Emirates. I can't tell you where I am exactly, because then I'd have to kill you. Our living conditions are great. We are near the coast, with air conditioning and three super meals a day. I even have a plastic pink pelican sitting out in front of my tent to remind me of home. You wouldn't believe the types of missions we are flying here. They're all very dangerous and I'm considered an easy target because of how low I have to fly. Did I ever tell you what I fly? (He didn't give me a chance to respond and he continued). . . . . I fly AWACS, did I tell you what that is? . . . ."

I couldn't let him rattle on, so I interceded with, "George, I'm glad to hear you're okay, but why are you calling me?"

"Because I wanted to tell you to try and get assigned to the Air Force because I know they'll have better living facilities." He then gave me his military TAC phone number so that I could call him from a military phone once I arrived in Saudi Arabia and tell him which military branch and what unit I'd be with. I didn't know what he was talking about regarding a TAC phone, but I figured I'd find out soon enough, if I went. I didn't want to tell him that I didn't understand what a TAC phone is, because then he'd go on forever about it.

"Okay, thanks for that information, but I don't think I'll have a choice as to which military branch I'll be attached to. So, how did you get my phone number?" I asked.

He said, "Oh, I looked it up in the phone book before I left and I tried calling you but you weren't home". He then hurriedly said he had to go because his time was up and again made sure I had his TAC phone number.

Next thing I knew, I realized I was in Saudi. I was no longer daydreaming. Nothing seemed to be going on; so then, I started thinking about my father. I actually started laughing to myself, because I knew that if my father were alive, he would rant and rave knowing that I had volunteered to go to Desert Shield. Dad always took pride in our military, but he always said he felt it was for men only. He had received a Purple Heart, a Bronze Star and several other medals during WWII while he served in the US Navy on the "flat top" Gambier Bay. His CVE 73 ship had been sunk during the Leyte Gulf Battle and he saw many men die. Though my father, Carl Robert Amos, didn't talk much about his experience in WWII, he would point out that he was a Taffy III survivor. Whatever that meant. It was like pulling teeth to get him to go into any detail.

I knew that my brothers and sisters and I were raised with a strong demeanor, that the military is the "backbone of America." At the moment, I knew how fortunate we were because the American people were in support of us, unlike the lack of support during Vietnam. I could only hope that the support of the American people would continue once the War started.

I then started laughing to myself because I knew my father would have been mad at me for even contemplating on being here. He was somewhat of a male chauvinist and felt that a woman's place is in the home and not in the work force with men. Needless to say, Dad and I got into several arguments in the past about men's roles versus women's roles. All of a sudden, a warm feeling came over my entire body as I was thinking of my father, and I believe he was up there, in heaven, watching my every move.

When I left for ODS (Operation Desert Shield) training in January 1991, my kid brother Daniel was on stand-by, ready to deploy himself. He was in the ARMY National Guard out of Casa Grande, Arizona, on a 24 hr standby ready to deploy at a moment's call. Daniel specialized in tank mechanics and retrieval. He hadn't planned on ever being deployed to "war" outside of our United States. He believed his training was to defend our home front and though he would be shipped off to another Country to fight their war, he told me he was ready to perform his duties as requested, though he didn't agree with the mission changing to defend another Country's territory. I ended up leaving Arizona before him and didn't know if he was still on hold or if he was on his way to Saudi Arabia. When I told him about my volunteering to go and being accepted, he laughed and said, "Well Sis, someone has to do the job and I'm very proud of you. I just wish it was someone else instead of you." I promised him that as soon as I found out where I was located in the Gulf region that I would try to let someone in our family know, so that if he hadn't left yet, then he'd know where I was at, or a general idea, when he deployed.

My other brother, Paul, was in the US Navy serving in Sigonella, Sicily and was sent to the Persian Gulf area August the 9th, 1990 the day President Bush stated, "A line has been drawn in the sand." I'll never forget that day and those words. The deployments soon started and the name, Desert Shield, soon evolved. When I told people that my brother was in the Navy and on the ground somewhere in the Persian Gulf region, they would look at me quizzically and ask, "I thought you said he was in the Navy, so how can he be on the ground?" Paul was a petty officer in the Helicopter Combat Support Squadron (HC4) as a detachment for the 1st Marine Division. He flew CH-53E Super Stallion helicopters for the Navy Seals. He was in recognizance and no telling what his mission was or where he was at exactly. He could be in Iraq behind enemy lines, in Saudi Arabia or in Kuwait. I knew he was out there somewhere, in danger's path. He had called home for Thanksgiving and I told him that I had volunteered with the American Red Cross to go to Desert Shield and perform emergency communications and short-term counseling.

He was shocked. He said, "I was wondering if you'd heard anything about Daniel, if he was going with the National Guard. I can't believe that I may have a sister over here also. Now I'm going to have to worry about you too!" He had once told me that one of the reasons he went to Vietnam and was a lifer in our armed forces was to keep us safe and out of harms way. He always said that he'd much rather go overseas and fight in order to keep other countries free and safe, to prevent war ever reaching America. Having served in Vietnam, he knew how horrible war was and never wanted us to face it in America. I admired my brother and my father and had a lot of respect for them, for loving our Country and our family.

All of a sudden, Paul started laughing and said, "Is this a joke? Are you joking me? Just think Sis, I'm the black sheep, ready to go to war and kill, and then there's you, the white sheep, not carrying a weapon, counseling and passing emergency messages in a war zone which you may be killed in." Paul was laughing so hard that he could hardly talk. After taking a few deep breaths and settling down a bit, he then said, "I don't think the Arab countries are ready for you. You might have a hard time dealing with their way of living and treating women. Leave them alone! Ya know, if you think Dad was chauvinistic, you're going to be in for a big surprise when you get here."

Paul couldn't tell me where he was located other than giving me an

FPO mailing address. He told me to make sure that I take an AT&T calling card with me, and that once I arrive in theater, that I would need to get to an AT & T telephone, which were located everywhere, even on the front. . . . and for me to call mom or our older sister Carol and advise them what military organization I was assigned to. He knew I would not be assigned to the Navy, because Red Cross was not allowed on ships. Emergency messages intended for the Navy was passed through telephonically to their Chaplain or Commander on their ship out of our EMERCOM that was in Washington, D.C. He thought I might be assigned to the Marines on the ground. By my providing my sister the military organization I would be attached to, he felt he could probably find out the area I would be located in.

"Well, sis, if you're assigned to the Marines or Army, you're going to have the surprise of your life. Well, I don't know when I can call you again, and it looks like my time has run out, so you take care and I love ya." He knew my mind was made up, and he knew how ignorant I was regarding military living, thinking, strategy, dress, talk, and everything else. I knew, that when he hung up the phone, that he would go back to his mates and tell them about his dumb sister and rant and rave like my father would have, yet I knew he loved me.

The only thing I knew was that if I was offered a chance to go and assist, I was ready. I needed to start a new chapter in my torn life. So much had happened to me. . . . .and then my mind wandered off in another direction . . . reminiscing about the events that led me to Desert Storm.

LIFE EVENTS LEADING ME TO DESERT STORM

I was a middle child, born in Safford, Arizona in 1952 to two Oakies from Stigler, Oklahoma. My father was very domineering, and my mother was always concerned about the house and how we girls kept our hair. I was the youngest daughter, with two older sisters and one older brother. Then, there were my two younger brothers. . . . Paul and Daniel. Oh yes. Paul. My brave Navy brother. I remember when we were small, and we all dressed up wearing mom's dresses and high heels. Paul and Daniel (my baby brother who is now in the Army National Guard) were fun until they got bigger and were able to beat me up. All three of us would jump off of our one-car garage acting like Superman. I've told my brothers that it's because of the proper training I gave them growing up as to why they grew up strong and brave. Paul would just laugh at me while Daniel was always the quiet one. I guess with five older siblings, anyone would be quiet.

I didn't play much with my older siblings. Donnie, the oldest, tried playing with me when I was young and my arm was pulled out of the socket when he was swinging me around. Boy did he get in a lot of trouble. Donnie never wanted to play with me anymore after that, but he was good at scaring me when Boris Karlof or Christopher Reeves would play in the old scary movies. *Dracula, The Werewolf, The Mummy.* He'd sneak up on me while I was covering my eyes, and then he'd yell and jump. I hated that.

My oldest sister, Carol, I could always depend on. She was always there when I needed her, but she and Shirley, my other sister, were so close in age, that they were always competing with each other. Especially when it came to boys.

I remember when I was about 13, both of my sisters were sitting on the front porch of our small home and they were talking about boys and the fun of kissing. I spoke up saying how it was gross and my darling sister Carol, said, "Do you know how men and women have sex?"

I was very naïve, because I didn't even know what "sex" meant. Shirley started laughing and next thing I knew, they both blended in telling me all about it. It sounded so gross and I swore I would never have anything to do with boys. Especially because I saw how they were always fighting each other over what boy was taking them out and the competition involved. Shirley developed very quickly which added to the arguments. You'd think the oldest sister would be larger busted, but not so. Though there were two years difference between them, Shirley was much more developed.

Me, I was in a training bra until I married at the young age of 17 to my high school sweetheart-Don Evans. Don and I met on a blind date when I was 15 years of age. My family and I had just moved to Winkelman and my brother introduced me to a gal from Kearny. She set up the blind date with Don, and from that point on; we were crazy about each other. We had dated for two years and decided to get married once he graduated and gained employment at Kennecott Copper Mines.

We had our first son, Don Evans Jr. the following year. A year later I gave birth on Mother's Day to a stillborn daughter. This was a very heart breaking and horrible experience and was totally unexpected. Back then; they didn't have the equipment or technique to determine if there was anything wrong.

This encouraged me to turn to God. Fortunately, I had been a

Christian since I was young, and loved the Lord wholeheartedly. This saddened loss of a daughter, brought me even closer to God.

A year later, I gave birth to another son, Wayne Edward Evans. Five years later, I had a miscarriage, and decided to not have any more children.

We stayed very busy with our lives and started a "side" business of pumping septic tanks, one-year after we were married. We would make a joke when friends called and when asked what we were doing we'd say, "Oh, we're talking about shit!"

When Wayne reached preschool age, I decided to obtain my GED and attended college eventually obtaining a Business/Office Education Associate in Applied Science Degree. It took a long time, but I finally finished.

After ten years, we moved to St. Johns, Arizona where Don gained employment with Salt River Project as a diesel mechanic. We took our side business of pumping out septic tanks and expanded it to include more than 100 portable toilets, which he serviced and set up on construction sites.

During the next 11 years, I worked at several places, and slowly worked into some great positions. My various work experience during this time consisted of being a Medical Assistant, Secretary, Personnel Assistant for Brown and Root, Inc., Chiropractic Assistant, CTI trucking secretary, Chief Deputy Clerk of Superior Court, Satellite Manager for Northland Pioneer College, and an instructor for them for approximately six years. I taught in Show Low, St. Johns, Springerville, and the most exciting teaching job was on the Whiteriver Apache Indian Reservation. I taught secretarial type classes in the community.

I was a mover and a motivator and was very outspoken. I became involved in our local Chamber of Commerce and served on the Board as their Secretary. I helped establish the Economic Development Corporation in St. Johns and was one of the signers of the Articles of Incorporation. I was a board member of the Navopache Business & Professional Working Women in America in Pinetop for the White Mountain Region. I had been asked to serve on the Northeastern Division of the United Way. I had been a Den Mother for the cub scouts, an interview Judge for Region I Academic Decathlon, and a member of the Apache County Private Industry Council.

With all of this going on, we still made time for our sons who were either involved in gymkhana, horseback riding, rodeos, roping, hunting, fishing, or motor cross racing.

I'm not saying that we had a perfect marriage, because there were definite problems in our family, which all pointed to drinking. With so much going on in our lives, we both preoccupied ourselves with things to do. He had his side business, and I was involved with organizations and continuing my education.

Next thing I knew, on Easter Sunday, April 3rd 1988, tragedy hit and Don was killed instantly in a vehicle accident. I was in shock. I couldn't believe this had happened. I kept telling myself that it was a bad dream and I'd wake up soon. Finally reality hit. He was dead.

My oldest son, Don Jr. was 18 years old and due to graduate from high school in one month. He hung in there and graduated.

Wayne was 16 ½ years old, and was a sophomore in high school.

Time slowly crept by, and Wayne became a nightmare. We made it through the summer after his father's death, but emotionally Wayne was torn and he had a hard time holding it together. Wayne's first semester as a junior in high school consisted of straight D's and soon F's. He had started running around with the wrong type of boys and his whole attitude had changed. I took him in for counseling, and was told to either find a man because Wayne needed a father image, or move somewhere else where we could start over. I chose the latter.

We moved to Tucson the early part of 1989 and Wayne became much more incorrigible and did things I never thought I'd ever see one of my sons' do. I soon found out what 'tuff love' was all about, and my next book will be called, "I Love You, but I Don't Like You".

Don Jr. went one semester to the local community college and then decided to go to UTI School in Phoenix where he decided to earn a two-yr. degree in Diesel Mechanics. He also met a young gal whom he decided he wanted to marry.

I, in the meantime, decided to become a realtor, and after going to real estate school, I obtained my realtor's license and went to work for

Denton Real Estate. I soon discovered that being a realtor isn't all fun. In fact, there's a lot of boring stuff that has to get done in order to finally close on a home. I sold a couple of homes, but needed something else in my life, so I volunteered at the local LaCholla Nursing Home reading to old people and doing their nails.

I also volunteered for the American Red Cross in Disaster Services after undergoing several classes through the Tucson Red Cross Chapter.

In addition to this, I decided to find a "fun" job and soon gained employment as a Personnel Assistant with Pima County Human Resources.

By mid 1990, Wayne was no longer living at home. He was in Phoenix and, "on his own". I was alone; except for my two dogs Patches and Brandy, and my two horses, Comanche and Peaches. So many things had happened in such a short time. Oh, I had dated a few times, but I wasn't ready for any type of a relationship. I hadn't met anyone I cared to spend much time with. In fact, I had met a lot of jerks and I just didn't have time or patience to deal with that type of person, even though some were in prominent positions. I had also met a couple of nice guys, but I just wasn't ready for any type of commitment. I found that it was difficult trying to be "just friends" with men.

Then, August 9, 1990, Iraq invaded Kuwait and the next thing I knew my brother Paul called me and said he was on his way to the Persian Gulf area. All of a sudden, I had this overwhelming feeling that I needed to go too. I knew that if they reinstated the draft that it was inevitable that one of my sons would be over there. I had no one at home to worry about, and if I lost my life, I wouldn't be leaving any minor children behind or a husband. I had always taken pride in our country, and maybe this was the one way I could show support for our military. So, for the love of my country, I immediately called the American Red Cross in Tucson and told them I was volunteering to go to the Persian Gulf because I knew the Red Cross would need caseworkers in emergency communications in the field attached to the military. I started volunteering at the Tucson American Red Cross Chapter as a caseworker in Services to Military Families and Veterans, and sent a letter

November 8, 1990 to the American Red Cross National Headquarters in Washington, D.C. volunteering to go, without pay, wherever they needed me. I barely had enough money to keep my bills going for a year without causing a hardship on me, but I knew I could make it.

I spoke to my employer, Pima County Human Resources, and asked them for a leave of absence if I was chosen to provide emergency communication services in the Gulf region. They approached the Board of Supervisors and returned with, "Yes, Barbara, you will be given a one-year leave of absence if you are requested to be deployed, but we need to make sure you are aware that the leave of absence is "without pay and without benefits". We are overwhelmed with your bravery in volunteering to go to an area full of danger, just for your country. We wish you a safe return."

Then, I received a call from Red Cross headquarters and they were prepared to interview me. This was when I flew to California and met George on the plane. Within a week after my return from the interview, I received a phone call saying I was selected, but I had to undergo and pass several types of training.

I was now ready to face a new challenge and a new way of living, eating, and thinking. I had no idea just how much my life was going to change.

INITIAL PREPARATIONS

On November 16, 1990, I received a letter from the American Red Cross National Headquarters in Washington, D.C. stating I had been selected to attend a training program for those who were being assigned to the Gulf. I had to first undergo extensive scrutiny, which included a national background check (NAC), and a complete physical.

Since I had earlier volunteered to go without pay, I asked them if this was the agreement.

I was told, "By Federal legislation, you must be paid when you are deployed in the line of danger. Also Barbara, the military is being paid." I couldn't help but say, "Yes, but they are fighting, putting their life on the line, where I am a noncombatant."

"You are correct in that sense, but do you realize that you are also in a field of danger and can die just as easily? Do you know how many Red Cross personnel we lost in Vietnam? Five to be exact and several more were wounded. No one is out of harm's way when you are at war or in an area which is hostile."

The very next day I received by Federal Express, a Defense Industrial Security Clearance Office (DISCO) form to fill out in order for them to conduct the NAC and obtain a Secret clearance in my name. I was shocked at the amount of questions they asked and the information I needed to furnish them. The information they required was unrelenting. Providing all names I used throughout my life was easy, but then when I had to list all addresses where I had lived, all schools I had attended, how many children I had, and information about them and my siblings and parents, I almost went nuts. I also had to provide all of my previous and present employment history. To try to remember what happened and all addresses during the past 38 years of my life was totally unexpected and it took a lot of phone calling and research to come up with the correct information.

I couldn't help but wonder if Congressmen were scrutinized like this before they took office.

Oh well, I endured the many pages full of questions about every second of my life, and returned them to the ARC headquarters within one week.

The next step was to undergo a complete physical that started from my head and went down to my small toe. I was beginning to wonder if my sister Carol had called them and told them that I had a screw loose for volunteering. Not only did they x-ray every part of my body and bend and poke me, but they also gave me a relentless amount of shots. I say relentless because both arms had to be used and I still wonder where they found enough flesh for as many shots as they gave me. I walked around like a zombie for the next two weeks with every part of my body aching.

In addition to this, I was required to take a First Aid and CPR (cardiopulmonary resuscitation) class from the American Red Cross. I needed to be certified to perform this type of assistance because there was an excellent chance that we would be utilizing it sometime in the near future after I arrived in the Gulf. My First Aid was current, but I had to update my CPR, which I did. Each time I breathed into the lifelike mannequins, I kept thinking that I would possibly be using this skill in the near future to save a life. My hands were shaking and I think I memorized the entire book.

I turned in my leave of absence request form to Pima County Human Resources and advised them that December 22, 1990 was going to be my last day at work. I was lucky because they were willing to allow me to take a leave of absence, which guaranteed me my position back. That is, if I returned. Upon leaving work that evening, I had dinner with a friend of mine. Her husband was a WW II veteran and he shared with me his feelings of anger toward the American Red Cross because they charged soldiers for coffee and refreshments during WWII. I was somewhat surprised and knew I needed to get the whole story regarding this, and who else, other than from the American Red Cross. I called Western Operations Headquarters in California and they shared the "rest of the story." The American Red Cross has gotten a bad rap for this since WW II and it was of no choice of the American Red Cross. They faxed me a copy of a letter signed by the Secretary of War telling the American Red Cross that they "had" to charge for these services, because the other Red Cross societies in Europe were charging money and we were making them look bad. So, we had no choice. I didn't hesitate to call my friend and share this information with her, which she was delighted to hear. She knew there had to be some reason behind it, though her husband was adamant that it was the American Red Cross' fault.

I was very fortunate to be able to spend Christmas with my family. I knew how many military dependants had to spend it alone, without their spouse, father, or sibling. They didn't know whether they would ever get to see their loved one again. The heartache, worry, and loneliness were their only constant companions.

Meanwhile, work at the American Red Cross Tucson Chapter continued to increase. There were all kinds of emergency situations happening with family members of the military. Our job was to verify the emergency and family relationship and see if the doctor recommended the service member's presence and if so, "why". It had to be provided in 'lay men's' terms as to what the exact diagnosis was along with the prognosis of the emergency situation. We would then send the message to our EMERCOM in Washington, D.C. who would forward it to our staff deployed in the Gulf. Our Red Cross staff who were already deployed in the Gulf, then had to find where the service member was located and pass the message to the appropriate Commander or First Sergeant. Then the American Red Cross would send us a response as to what action the military was taking in regards to emergency leave for the service member. This all took time.

Sometimes I wondered why it took so long to get a response. We were, by regulation, supposed to have some type of an answer within 24 hours but that never happened. I couldn't wait to get to Saudi Arabia and find out what was causing the delay.

The mental anguish our dependent spouses and children were going through was tremendous. It didn't help to watch CNN and hear about the statistics of how many American military members were predicted to die once the ground and air war started. Every moment at home was spent in front of the television. I didn't want to miss any breaking news.

My mother was worried about my brother Paul who was already over there, and she knew Daniel was on stand-by, ready to deploy. I knew she was upset that I was leaving. She didn't want three of her children over there. Especially one of her daughters. I knew we weren't the only families with more than one family member over there. It was as if we were all on a roller coaster never knowing which way it was going to go or "who" wouldn't be coming back alive.

Western Operations Headquarters called me and said that I needed to make travel arrangements to arrive at Ft. Sam Houston, Texas on January 3, 1991 and the next thing I knew, I was on my way.

SAM HOUSTON—
THE FIRST TRAINING

Upon arriving in San Antonio, Texas, I was greeted by ARC staff and taken to a hotel room that I shared with another Red Cross volunteer named Karen. Karen was glad to be there, but didn't quite know if she wanted to go forward. The reality was just hitting her about going to War and being in a place where she might die and never see her family again. She had decided to continue with the training, and make a final decision. Afterwards, we went to a "welcome dinner" which was the first gathering for approximately 40 Red Cross personnel who were all volunteers, ready to go through this stage of training. Everyone was eager and nervous at the same time thinking about the challenge that lay ahead and wondering if we were all going to return.

What was interesting was how different we all were. Some were previous Vietnam veterans. Some were young adults. Several were in my age group, middle aged. Some had been volunteers with the American Red Cross for quite a awhile. One guy was a preacher and said he felt he was needed there. One young gal by the name of Diane, said her fiancé' was a local national in Kuwait and she was worried about him and wanted to get over there to "help" the cause. Another gal said she was a Jew and felt that her duty was to assist those who protect Israel. One gal's mother was already over there with the Red Cross. There were many reasons and I felt that if I had a good reason, they all had good reasons for going.

Early the next morning in class we were given forms to fill out stating we understood that our deployment could last up to one year. Several people disagreed with this because originally, most of us were told to plan on six months. So, we all signed off and those who wanted to change it to six months were allowed to. After all, some of us had leave of absences from our current jobs, but some were only for six months.

Once our training started, one of the first things explained to us were the different divisions the American Red Cross has, and how each operate under different laws, guidelines, and funding. I knew about the Disaster Division, because I had been a disaster volunteer and had gone out on two assignments. I assisted one family whose home had been flooded, and the other one was a family of four whose home had burned down leaving them without food and a roof over their head. They knew Red Cross was a blessing to come to their aid; especially when they found out they didn't have to pay any of the assistance back. Disaster relief is always grant free and consists of food, shelter, clothing, and other assistance depending on each situation.

We were informed that the Blood Division operates under their own funding and guidelines and that they were currently shipping more than 1,000 units of blood to the Persian Gulf Region each week. This could not have happened without the on-going support of Americans who unselfishly donated their blood.

The Health & Safety Division we were told, offers a variety of classes throughout the local community and on military bases, which partly consists of swimming, First Aid, CPR, HIV and many other types of classes. These classes are offered throughout all communities throughout the states.

Finally, we discussed our division SAF (Services to the Armed Forces), which is now known as Armed Forces Emergency Services. These are located on military bases, and the SMF & V (Services to Military Families and Veterans) within the local communities in Chapters.

All of these divisions have been mandated through Congress since 1905 to undertake relief activities for the purpose of mitigating the suffering caused by separation and disaster. This is where The Red Cross authority to perform emergency communications comes from. A Congressional charter had been granted to the American Red Cross that required the organization to act "in accord with the military authorities as a medium of communication between the people of the United States and their Armed Forces . . ." These emergency communications exist between loved ones in the community and abroad on military bases, including deployed areas—all of which I was there to train for.

Different National Societies throughout the world provide one or more types of services. The American Red Cross nurses and ambulance drivers served during the Spanish-American War and World War I. The Red Cross canteens welcomed American troops during World War II, and American Red Cross recreation clubs were established close to the front lines in the Korean and Vietnam conflicts. The Red Cross was now providing service members and their families with financial assistance, crisis intervention, support groups and a variety of other services.

I think the most important thing, was to differentiate the Societies and what they provide, in relation to the ICRC (International Committee of the Red Cross). This wonderful committee based out of Geneva, Switzerland is the father and founder of the Geneva Conventions also known as the International Humanitarian Laws. The first Geneva Convention was first signed in 1864 and now has four Conventions with some 400 articles and two Protocols. The Geneva Conventions has laws, which if abided by, alleviate the sufferings of all the victims of armed conflicts who are in the power of their enemy, whether wounded, sick or shipwrecked, prisoners of war or civilians. There are civilians, combatants, and non-combatants. Most countries, including third-world countries signed and adopted most of these articles. Iraq, other Arab Countries, Israel, NATO members, and the United States have all signed some of these. The governments are then held accountable for any violation.

Each Country's Red Cross Society (such as the American Red Cross) fall under the ICRC and the services provided are specifically for humanitarian purposes, but at different levels, according to what each society can afford to provide.

We were given a handout educating us about the Geneva Conventions explaining our rights and the enemy's rights and equality of protection under specific guidelines for our armed forces, POW's, and civilians. This included protection of medical personnel and transportation, protection of the Red Cross and other relief society emblems, and protection of civilians who were non-combatants.

Because of my family who had served in Vietnam, I had to ask "Where was the ICRC when it came to Vietnam?" I had one brother, and two brothers-in-law's who had served there. One brother-in-law had been wounded in Vietnam but served his year and then volunteered and returned to Vietnam for a second term. I remembered in our talks one specific comment, "Where was the ICRC in Vietnam?" and feel it appropriate to ask, "Will they be there for us in this war?" The answer was short and to the point, "We were there, but we were limited because both sides had violated the treaties and neither side would stop what they were doing."

We were told that Iraq is a signee of the treaties and will be held accountable. All Countries will be held accountable if they break this binding agreement. There is no way of saying whether one country will live up to the Geneva Conventions, but only through experience. We can only hope they will live up to their promises which they've all agreed upon."

In addition to this, the ICRC provides tracing services, which tries to find those family members who are missing and exchanges family messages between people separated by armed conflict. When I was in Tucson, one caseworker was assisting an older couple in trying to find her brother who had been missing since WWII. She knew he was taken to a concentration camp and had never heard from him since. She was now dying of cancer and the "not knowing" had always weighed heavily on her mind. She was searching for an end to her mental suffering. She just wanted to know–"was he gassed or shot, or by some miracle, did he survive. If he died, which concentration camp did he die in?" This research, which we were just starting, was going to take quite a bit of time because of where it had to go. The process was all time consuming. It was doubtful if an answer would be back in time before she died, but we were going to give it our best shot.

Our next training was the most important. It was casework training, which we would be providing to all military personnel and civilians in the Gulf region.

As of December 27, 1990 there had been some 64,000 emergency messages transmitted to service personnel between the Gulf and their families in the United States. The Red Cross' emergency communications service is the only round-the-clock, round-the-world network that allows service members to stay in touch with their families about births, deaths, and serious illnesses. We were now going to be performing casework in SAF (Services to the Armed Forces), which meant we were no longer based in a local city or community, but on a military base in a deployed status. Our part was not only in transmitting the message, but it was providing enough information to the military so an immediate decision could be made as to whether the emergency warranted emergency leave for the service member. This was not ARC's decision. The military Commanders would make all leave decisions.

We were also expected to be there as a support for our soldiers in helping them keep a positive attitude, no matter how bad things turned.

As of January 4, 1991, 63 Red Cross workers were in the Persian Gulf area processing these messages. They had plans on having approximately 154 in place by March 1, and I was going to be one of the first recruits to arrive. I was in the first group of American Red Cross volunteers to undergo an extensive training conducted by the Red Cross in conjunction with the US military. ARC had hopes that we would be in theater by the end of January because they had several other groups of people they were trying to get ready to undergo this same training. The personnel currently in theater were swamped with work and needed assistance. I was eager to get it over with and get there . . . where we were desperately needed.

Next, we were to pass the psychological test; learn Red Cross casework skills in a deployed status with unforeseeable obstacles; familiarize ourselves with the history and customs of Saudi Arabia; and learn military survival skills so we could come back alive.

A couple of people in the group did not make it beyond the psychological test. There were quite a few dumb questions on the written test, and it made me think they were trying to trick you. In particular, one question was asked, "How often do you dream of sex?" then it was addressed another way, "Which of the following do you dream the most of–and you would pick your answer. One selection was "sex". There were several other questions, which they would turn around and ask again, just differently.

When score results were not favorable, then the individual would have to go speak to a professional counselor who would then make the decision as to whether this person could handle a war zone, high stress and demands with long hours.

Then we had to undergo a lot of intensive casework training in a short period of time. The American Red Cross was operating under Minimize Conditions. This condition was imposed by the Joint Chiefs of Staff related to the "types of emergency messages" which were allowed to be transmitted and passed in the field. The only messages allowed were those pertaining to births, deaths, and critical illnesses. We were going to be dealing directly with the soldiers, their 1SGs, and their Commanders in processing these messages and notifying the service members as to the crisis with a return response. Soldiers would be coming to us needing help and we would have to be prepared to gather enough information from the soldier to send an inquiry which would involve all needed verification so the soldier could take leave, or at least know the "true story" of what was happening. A soldier may have received a letter from home with bad news or they called home and were told that there was a crisis. Our mission was to get as much information as possible so the military could make a decision regarding emergency leave.

With this information, we would need to send a message out of theater using military communications. These communication devices would vary throughout theater and the only way of preparing for these devices was by doing it. Being there and dealing with it. This sounded quite easy, but little did I know the true extent of communication problems we would encounter in the field.

In order to expect a fast response, we needed specific information in our message. The most important things to ask were the four WWWWs. Who, what, when and where. Who is ill or deceased, what is their relationship to you, how did this happen, when did this happen, where did this happen, where are they at, who can be contacted in the states for additional information, is a doctor involved. . . . and any other information which would help.

Then, we learned how to send a message using the appropriate format with the required information of the service member which consisted of their name, rank, social security number, branch of service, and unit address, APO or FPO. When we sent a message out of theater, we had to remember to ask the doctor or family member "why" they were requesting the soldier's presence. Then, once a response was returned to us with all of the information needed, all we had to do was deliver it to the soldier.

This sounded fairly easy, but once I was deployed and experienced the living and working conditions, I soon found out how difficult this mission was.

Those of us who passed the American Red Cross casework training were to attend classes conducted by the military the next day. These classes consisted of war-related stress; combat casualty symptoms and reactions; mental health roles in mass casualty and disaster operations; terrorism; and military courtesy.

After today's training, we all went out for dinner and went on the "River Walk" in San Antonio. It was enjoyable until I met some ole fart that was sitting out on a patio having a drink. He saw my Red Cross insignia and asked me if I was a volunteer there. When I proceeded to tell him that I was undergoing training for deployment, he laughed and said, "Oh yeah, I remember you Red Cross people real well. You were right there with us in Vietnam making good money off of us guys by selling your services day and night. A lot of Red Cross women left there with a lot of money."

I could have crawled into a hole. I felt violated and was angry that he would base my morals on him or other people. I didn't know what happened in Vietnam, and I didn't appreciate him trying to make assumptions about me or anyone else.

I quickly responded. "You have no right to judge me on your past experiences. I'm sure you don't feel the men who visited these women were morally wrong, do you?" Without waiting for a response from him, I quickly walked off and went back to my hotel room.

I couldn't wait until Karen returned so I could blow off steam. After pacing back and forth and being upset for two hours, we finally hit the sack and woke up early the next morning ready to start the military classes, the first one being on stress, which I needed at the time.

Classes started at 0730 a.m. on January 9 by a Colonel Adams, Ph.D. We were told the following: "War related stress is not just for the soldier but also involves the loved ones back home. Stress is a unique and personal response from our bodies and minds to meet the demands that different situations give to us. These situations–such as concern for a loved one in the Persian Gulf, the constant exposure to violence by media coverage of the war or the fear of terrorism here– trigger an instinctive "fight or flight" response. Stress affects everyone differently. Some stress is normal, but the most important stress to watch out for is negative stress. Some symptoms are persistent fatigue, inability to concentrate, flashes of anger which causes you to lash out at friends and family, changes in eating and sleeping habits, increased use of alcohol, tobacco, etc., prolonged tension headaches, lower back aches, stomach problems or other physical ailments, and prolonged feelings of depression, anxiety or helplessness. The different ways to cope with stress are; talk it out, try physical activity, know your limits and make time for relaxation, take control by volunteering or writing letters, and avoid self-medication such as excessive caffeine, nicotine, and alcohol. Alcohol in theater will not be an issue for it is not allowed in Saudi Arabia." We then learned several quick relaxing techniques that can be done anywhere at any time.

Then we were told about the combat casualty symptoms, known as "battle fatigue". "There are various symptoms to look for. Physical signs consist of tension head and backache, trembling, fumbling, jumping, pounding heart, breathing too rapidly, upset stomach, diarrhea, fatigue, weariness, distant, and a haunted (1,000 yard) stare. Mental and emotional signs are anxiety, worrying, irritability, swearing, complaining, difficulty concentrating, remembering, communicating, awakened by bad dreams, grieving, feeling guilty, anger at own one's own team, losing confidence in self and unit. Most serious are those who flinch or duck at most sudden sounds and movement, shaking of arms or whole body, cowering in terror, parts of body won't work right without apparent physical reason, rapid talking, freezing under fire, arguing and starting fights, deliberately reckless action, no interest in food or anything else, seeing or hearing things which are not really there, and so on. One of the most important things to remember is that sleep and physical activity is essential to keep mentally fit. Keep everyone informed and control rumors. Talk. Keep the team focused on the mission and how to succeed. If it is brought to your attention of someone whom you feel is suffering serious battle fatigue symptoms, tell the leader and stay positive."

"One of the most important things to remember about mental health and casework roles is that once the soldier or client has suffered serious combat stress, they react differently. They may have vehement anger, profuse profanity or a severe antisocial conduct. They are not doing this because of 'you' but because of what they have experienced. Make sure their leader or medical personnel are informed of the soldier so help can be ascertained right away."

The information provided about 'terrorism' was very interesting. We were told, "Personal protective measures against terrorism are essential both at home, and abroad. Terrorism at home could be anywhere. Always remember to keep a low profile. Shun publicity. If the news media interviews you, do not give your address or family information, because terrorists are known to strike anyone at any time. Avoid public disputes and get into the habit of 'checking in' to let your friends and family know where you are or when to expect you. Vary your times and routes from work and arriving home."

I remembered when I was in Tucson and attended a County Supervisors' meeting how well prepared they were. They had told the public that every state in the Union was watching their dams, electrical power plants, water resources, nuclear generating stations, and airports for terrorists with 24-hour coverage each and every day. It was amazing to hear how every town and state came together with terrorist preparation to hopefully avoid the worst from happening

"For those deployed, terrorists usually look for easy targets and people who use the same route. If for any reason you hear a loud noise, quickly grab your sleeping bag and roll out of your bed to one side. If there is shrapnel, hopefully it will lodge into your bag. If there is no noise but a bright light—get behind an object because it is probably a nuclear weapon. Use common sense."

A question I asked, which was weighing heavily on my mind was, "So what about our soldiers when they are having to work side by side with known terrorist countries? It's bad enough that they have to worry about the front, chemical warfare, and scuds, but now they have to watch their side also?"

I was quickly told, "they will not be fighting side by side in combat. Each country will be well defined and located in their own area. The amount of their weapons and soldiers is nothing in comparison to ours, and we have to trust our government and the decisions they make."

I remembered how our government neglected to admit to the Agent Orange contamination in Vietnam. For some reason, I felt a little uncomfortable with that statement.

One of the most chilling moments before I departed for the Gulf was when we were told to make sure our wills and POA's (power of attorneys') are up to date for our family members if something happened to us.

Finally we discussed military courtesy. Here we learned the military titles and a list of ranks, which accompanied them. I don't know who decided that a LTC (Lieutenant Colonel) with a silver clover is supposed to be higher than a Major with a gold clover. For those of us who are not accustomed to military ranks, and for those of us who are female, "gold is always worth much more than silver". So why on earth they decided a LTC should have a clover of silver is beyond me. I really had a hard time looking at a gold clover and remembering that this person is beneath a silver clover in rank. I could understand the "birds" on a full-bird colonel's shoulders and understood that this was a higher rank, because eagles always soar high. (At least in my mind).

The packet stated when and where to salute, but since we were civilians, we were not supposed to salute. We were informed that we were going to be issued military uniforms. This I found rather surprising, as I wasn't military. We were not told how to wear the uniform properly, and at this stage we were not issued any uniforms because we still had to complete our training and see if we were finally approved to deploy. We were told though, that we needed to be punctual, respectful, use common sense and good judgement in all things. Remember, rank has its privileges and since I was going to be performing as an Assistant Station Manager, my equivalency was going to be a Major (or a GS12 in Civil Service equivalency). Officers were afforded a little higher standard of living. I was going to find out that a tent is a tent and an MRE (meal ready to eat) is an MRE no matter who eats it or what rank you are.

Our last bit of training at Ft. Sam Houston consisted of the customs and courtesies of Saudi Arabia and a handout was given to us. We learned simple things, like don't cross your legs and point your toes toward an Arab because you are showing the bottom of your soles and it is an insult; Muslims' pray five times a day and it is piped throughout the community on speakers—no matter where they are or what they are doing, they will stop and get on their knees on a prayer rug facing the holy city of Mecca; never point nor bite your finger; do not give the sign "A-OK" because to an Arab, it symbolizes the sign of the evil eye; do not at any time discuss Israel; absolutely do not stare at, speak to, or pay any attention to veiled women or to people who are praying; and do not take pictures of women in their veils. Beware of all snakes and spiders and various insects. We were given handouts to take with us and read which proved to be very interesting.

Those of us who passed this training were going to be sent to strategic military bases to train with the American Red Cross SAF (Services to Armed Forces) stations, which were located in different states. This training was called "on-the-job" training that lasted approximately 10 days. I was told that I would be going to Ft. Lewis, Washington and was pretty excited, because I had never been there.

As I returned to my room and saw Karen, she informed me that she'd decided not to go. She had passed all of the training, but she had discussed it with her family and decided it was best to stay home, where it was safe. She had a husband and grandchildren that she loved very much and could not stand the thought of never seeing them again. She had been a volunteer for the Red Cross for several years and was going to continue helping, but here, in the States. She cried as she hugged me goodbye the next day. I could tell she felt as though she had deserted us and I told her how much I knew she was needed back home.

FT. LEWIS, WASHINGTON—ON THE JOB TRAINING

January 11, I arrived in Seattle, Washington and was greeted by Jan Santiago, the volunteer Training Coordinator for Western Operations Headquarters. She was very knowledgeable with American Red Cross procedures, specifically "emergency communications". She had been involved with the American Red Cross for over twenty years, where her husband was now a high ranking officer.

You know how you can sense when someone is the right person? I could tell right off that this short, Latin lady would become my shining idol mainly because of the way she carried herself with pride and complete confidence. My mother always told me that dynamite comes in small packages, and Jan was the proof. She informed me that myself and three others were arriving soon, and that we would be there a week to ten days.

We stayed at VIP quarters on base. The building we were in was huge and beautiful. There was a tremendously large fireplace in the reception room, and I loved relaxing there, drinking coffee and reading the paper.

The next day I met "Big Tom", who was a former Navy pilot, and had served in Vietnam. He showed me pictures of his grandchildren and said he was looking forward to going . . . he had volunteered like me, and something inside him was telling him that he needed to do this.

There was a guy name Russell, who had taken a leave of absence from his job, just like I had. He had never served in Vietnam and now he had a chance to do something. He wanted to make up for not serving in Vietnam, when all of his friends did.

Then I met Charisa. She too was from Arizona, and was looking forward to our adventure, like everyone else.

The first thing out of Jan's mouth was that the American Red Cross was caught with their pants down. In other words, they were not ready for this deployment for it was totally unexpected. They were doing as much as they could to find enough people who could pass all phases to send over. They had not seen action since Vietnam except in routine exercises, which was of course completely different. Red Cross staff had been sitting in positions for a long period of time and had not been mobile. Staff had not been required to undergo periodic physicals, so there were several who were not physically fit to go. The amount of staff needed for this massive deployment was two times the amount in comparison to the employees they actually had. All salaries were paid by donations and contributions provided by the American people. Now, they had to come up with the money to pay all of the additional employees' salaries. I discovered that the government does not fund any of the salaries. The need for volunteers was great and she appreciated us for coming forward and volunteering.

We were soon sitting with soldiers and family members counseling, referring and gathering important information in order to send emergency messages to those deployed. We gave financial assistance to those at Ft. Lewis who qualified in either a grant form or an interest free loan, which consisted of airline travel, hotel expense, meals, and other miscellaneous expenses.

Every break I took was spent in front of the television listening to CNN about Desert Shield and watching the scuds going into Saudi Arabia. Hundreds of thousands of soldiers had been deployed and many were still processing. The scare of chemical warfare on loved ones was very real and frightening for those family members left behind watching CNN. The emotional trauma families were feeling was day-by-day, minute-to-minute. Spouses were constantly hearing about how many people were projected to die. Mothers, without realizing the affect on their children, would start crying and pray out loud hoping that their daddy would be okay. This had a lasting impact on the children.

Many military couples were "both" soldiers and the father and mother of the children they had to leave. Many childcare plans became a nightmare. There was one situation where both parents were deployed and they had left their children with a close friend, because there were no relatives living close by. The close friend's father found out he had cancer and needed constant care, which was in another state. So, the close friend had to make emergency plans to leave and could not continue taking care of the children the military couple had left in their care.

Another major problem was with the single soldiers who had children. They were already struggling, trying to make it on the low military pay, now they had to survive with their children in someone else's hands 24 hrs a day, which in a lot of instances they had to pay for. They couldn't afford this. It's one thing to pay for childcare for 8 hours or while you're on regular duty, but when it's 24 hrs a day, 7 days a week—it becomes very expensive.

The military on the other hand had a mission that had to be done. After all, that's what the military is all about. To be sent at a moments call anywhere in the world.

In the meantime, everyone needed support and needed to hold together, which was almost impossible at times. That's what we were there for. To keep positive thoughts, support going, and provide necessary services to the soldiers and families no matter where they were located. Red Cross volunteers were set up at all deployment arenas handing out "comfort bags" and refreshments to all branches of the military as they were departing. The comfort bags consisted of donated items, such as comb, toothpaste, toothbrush, lotion, shampoo, Kleenex and a washcloth. These items eventually came in handy for those deployed.

Jan explained to us that our mission was to get all of the facts, or request all of the facts so a decision could be made. Too many times messages were sent from chapters who did not know how the military worked and they would not provide enough information for the military to make a decision regarding emergency leave. We needed to remember that we were staging for WAR and the mission to the military was the top priority.

Our purpose was to gather pertinent information and disseminate it to the appropriate people as soon as possible. There were so many cases, yet each was different. It made me realize what military families go through. I gained a lot of respect for the soldiers and especially for their families. The struggles and worries were a continuing complexity.

January 16, 1991 is a date I will never forget for three reasons. First, that's the day the Air War started and we progressed from Desert Shield to Desert Storm.

Secondly, that same day, I counseled and provided an Army soldier an emergency interest free loan to travel to Virginia because of the death of his mother. When I told him that the reason I was at Ft. Lewis was to undergo training in preparation for deployment to Desert Storm, he was surprised. He asked, "Have you ever been involved with the military before, or are you a military BRAT?"

I asked, "What exactly is a military brat? I've heard that phrase several times, but no one has explained it to me."

"It's someone who as a child was raised by a parent who either retired or served several years in the military."

"Oh", I said, "No, I'm not. My father was in the Navy, but he was out before I was even born. I've never lived around the military and this is turning into a real experience so far, but I'm determined that I'll make it."

He stated, "If you like privacy, you will not have it on a deployment. You might end up in an area where there are no toilets and the only thing you have is the shovel on your back. I would suggest your taking a shower curtain so you can drape it around you for privacy."

This piece of advice I quickly adhered to.

Thirdly, it was my sister Shirley's birthday, and I knew I would never forget that day.

January the 18th proved to be another interesting day. The first scuds hit Israel. Tariq Aziz lived up to his word when he had said earlier, "If Iraq is confronted in the Gulf, then Iraq will launch an unprovoked attack on Israel." Our Patriots were activated and destroyed many of the scuds, but some still landed in Israel.

There was one cruel result that came out of the use of the Patriots. Though the Patriots were useful in destroying the scuds, it was through their use that it was found to cause other problems. When they were utilized over urban areas, the destroyed debris would fall into these urban areas occasionally resulting in casualties of innocent people and buildings would be damaged.

Everyone was holding their breath to see if Israel was going to retaliate, which they were quite known for. We knew if that happened, the war would probably escalate, and other countries would get involved, causing our Country a possible World War. People would talk and wonder, "Is this going to be the end of the world as the Bible warns us of?"

I received a directive from National Headquarters stating that I was to plan on arriving in Columbia, SC on the 27th of January for final processing to the Persian Gulf. This was where I would get my final training and gear.

From Columbia, SC., I was to take a taxi to the Replacement Center at Ft. Jackson. I was to take my shot records with me, and boy was I glad to have that all over with (or at least I thought it was) and my HIV results.

Since I had a few days left here before going to South Carolina, I decided to purchase some desert colored military uniforms along with a duffel bag and some personal items. We had been advised of several personal items to take, but I soon found out that we were only allowed two duffel bags and a rucksack and any spare room was considerably limited because of all the room the military gear was going to use.

I remember driving all over the place trying to locate boots my size, and ended up having to purchase boots which were one size too big. I was told that an old Army trick was to soak your boots in hot water, and that would help shrink them to fit your feet. I also thought that if I wore thick enough socks, then I wouldn't have a problem. Time would only tell.

I was also required to take my dental x-rays with me along with my DNA to provide to the military in case I was a casualty and they needed to identify my remains.

My DISCO clearance and passport with VISAS were going to be at Ft. Jackson, our last stop, and I would be provided them there.

We were also informed that we needed to wear comfortable clothing and to be prepared for the military "in-processing".

This all sounded pretty easy and I couldn't wait to find out what military life was all about.

We took a break and it was showing on the news Iraqi launching scuds sporadically throughout Saudi and Israel. We were all at "awe" as we quietly sat and watched.

We returned for our training and Jan strongly cautioned us against "Loose lips. "Loose lips sink ships is what she said". Soldiers and family members were directed not to discuss certain information because it would possibly jeopardize operational security and troop safety. The most important things for us NOT to discuss were: do not discuss specific numbers of soldiers, supplies, and equipment in a unit; future plans; unit locations; rules of engagement; intelligence collection activities; unit movements, tactical deployments and dispersions; points of origin of aircraft; effectiveness of enemy camouflage, cover, deception, targeting, direct and indirect fire, security measures; missing or downed aircraft while search and rescue efforts are underway; Special Operations Forces methods, tactics, and unique equipment; specific operating methods such as angles of attack, speeds, and evasive maneuver techniques; and U.S. coalition vulnerabilities such as major battle damage or major personnel losses.

We were allowed to go home and see our relatives before we departed to Ft. Jackson, SC for deployment, but I chose not to. I had already said goodbye to my family and it was very difficult when I left, so I didn't want to put them nor me through that again.

Before departing for Ft. Jackson, I decided to cut my hair and nails short. I knew I wouldn't need any of that stuff since I was deploying, and I wanted the easiest way to care for myself.

IN-PROCESSING AT FT. JACKSON, SOUTH CAROLINA

Upon my arrival on Sunday, January 27 at Ft. Jackson, SC, there were several of the "old gang" there waiting. It had been since Ft. Sam Houston that we were all together. We were soon met by Red Cross staff and military personnel and were ushered by the military to WW II type vintage two-story wooden barracks.

We were told that our orders had been cut from the military stating we were to depart any time after the 27th of January for King Fahd International Airport in Saudi Arabia. We were there for the purpose of being "in-processed". At this time, we didn't know what "in-processing" meant, but we knew we'd be finding out soon.

The Red Cross staff who met us said that we were the very first Red Cross team to ever undergo "dual" training from ARC and the ARMY in preparation for war. There were now a total of 29 of us, and the military was going to take a group picture at the end of our training in our military uniforms which they were going to display at their Headquarters' office.

We were informed that while staying in our wonderful billeting, that each person had to pull "fire watch" for one hour during the night. Now, I didn't understand why we had to do this since there were smoke detectors in the building, but I did as told. I pulled my shift that night from 0130 a.m. until 0230 a.m. I then had to wake the next person up to pull their duty. We were all going to have to take turns each night until we departed for Saudi Arabia.

We started at the crack of dawn on Monday, January 28 standing in the long lines to be processed "in" and stamped "go" by all medical professions. I had already gone through this on the civilian side, but since I learned that the military is "in a world of their own". I knew I would still have to endure the lines and the "go" process.

Once one line was finished, we always had another one to go to. After passing the eye, dental, mental, and physical, we then had to go find the lines for the immunizations. I knew I had taken all of the shots required, but I still had to get stamped "go" before I could proceed to the next phase. As my turn arrived for the immunizations, I was informed that I needed at least four more shots. I couldn't believe it. Knowing that I was almost finished, I politely endured the shots and was prepared to suffer more soreness for the next few days. After all, compared to what we would endure in war, I knew this was going to be the easy part.

We soon discovered that the military ID cards that were issued to us were the wrong ones, for we were not military, but civilians. We were also given the wrong Geneva cards. The military had only one kind of Geneva Convention card and it was for combatants. Since we were non-combatants, our National Headquarters had to express mail the correct ones to the military for us.

We were then loaded up in buses and taken to warehouses, where we were issued military gear. We had printouts showing what we were going to be issued. There were two large computer pages. Each time one of the items listed was provided to us, they checked it off.

I never saw so much stuff and most of us had no idea what half of it was for. We were told that all of it had to go into two duffle bags and I just couldn't see how all of it could possibly fit into the duffle bags they gave us, so I asked if they had any larger ones and this one soldier issuing the supplies cracked up laughing. She was laughing so hard, that it made me laugh, though I didn't know why. She said, "Hey,

Sergeant, this Red Cross gal wants to know if we have larger duffle bags!" They both cracked up laughing and one of them went in the back and said she couldn't wait to tell the rest of the workers what I had asked for. I realized that the military had a keen sense of humor.

I quickly discovered that you take what the military gives you and don't ask questions. That was going to be hard for me.

After having all military gear signed out to us, we then had to lug it all back on the bus and head back to our barracks.

Upon returning to our barracks, the local Red Cross staff were there waiting for us. They informed us that they were having our nametags and badge made up, and that we would need to pin the badges to each one of our front pockets on each uniform. The name Red Cross was to be sewed on the right side above the pocket, and that with all of this identification, they felt that people could tell right away that we were not military. This supposedly could be identifiable at a short distance. We also were going to have "ARC" in a small square sewed onto each side of our collars.

I didn't understand why we were expected to wear military uniforms, so I asked them, "Would someone please explain why we have to wear military clothes? Isn't it important for us to be "obvious" to the military and other people that we are civilians as we were told during our Geneva Convention training at Ft. Sam Houston? Why can't we wear the Red Cross uniforms like they did in Vietnam and WWII"?

I was politely informed that since we were under the auspice of the military that we had to abide by their orders, and they said all civilians were to be issued uniforms for their protection. If civilians wore different clothing other than a military uniform, then they would be obvious targets for terrorists and the military did not want to take that chance.

We then started looking at the military gear, which had been issued to us, and tried to figure out what some of the stuff was. I realized that we had been issued cold weather gear. I kept thinking, "We're going to the desert where it's HOT, why on earth do we need this stuff for Eskimos?" I later appreciated having it.

Next, we were shuffled off for gas mask fitting. It was vital that we were fitted properly because of the chemical warfare threat. One small break in the seal of the gas mask would be life threatening. Later that evening we collapsed in our bunks at about 2300 hours (11:00 p.m.).

Tuesday, January 29 was training for the gas mask. We were taught how to put it on, how to clear it, and how to seal it so gas would not be able to come in. We had to hold our breath for quite some time while we were grabbing it out of our pouch, take it apart, clear it, seal it, and breathe.

We then went to the range and were put through the gas chamber. The military had never allowed "civilians" to go through the gas chamber before. They were concerned as to "who" would be responsible if something happened to one of us from this experience. The enlisted soldiers thought that their "heads would roll" if something happened to any of us, so we had to wait until higher officials gave the go-ahead. This made me think, "This must be pretty dangerous for them to be this concerned."

The word finally came down line allowing us to go through it, but they were not allowed to put us through testing as "extensive" as the military had to undergo.

As I was waiting in line to go forward into the gas chamber, I'll never forget watching a young soldier come running out of the back end of the building. He was pulling his mask off, gasping for air and choking. His face was beat red. A Sergeant started yelling at him and grabbed him, making him go back in. He stressed the importance of how he MUST seal his gas mask where no gas could get in, in order to survive under a chemical attack. I felt sorry for the soldier, but I respected the Sergeant for making him learn to do it the right way. It might save his life later.

After seeing this young man come out with a red face, and yelling, I realized this testing was probably not going to be the most pleasant part of my training. Upon going into the chamber with the gas mask on, a soldier walked up to each of us and broke our seal by lifting the gas mask up over our nose. If we breathed, he'd know it because it would make you sick and choke. It immediately started stinging my face and I grabbed the gas mask, cleared it and sealed it, all while holding my breath.

We then had to stand there until the soldier felt we were breathing on our own without any gas getting inside. This meant we had sealed the gas mask properly. He then allowed us to leave the chamber. I did not hesitate to get out and as soon as we hit fresh air, our masks came off. My cheeks were red from when they popped my gas mask up and the chemical hit my cheeks. It felt as though something was stinging my cheeks the whole time since the gas mask had been popped. I was so glad to have that part over with.

Upon returning to our barracks we were issued our MOPP gear. I never found out what MOPP meant, other than knowing it consisted of the clothing you'd put on to protect the rest of your body from exposure to chemicals. We were fitted and had to wear the bulky clothing including our gas mask for more than 1 ½ hrs to make sure no one was claustrophobic.

You know how people who go to the moon wear those long bulky outfits? That's exactly like what we looked like.

We were then informed that we would be leaving the very next morning. I called my sister Carol to see how my family, my dogs, and my horses were doing. She said that George had called her again to see if she had heard anything from me. She thought he sounded pretty neat, but I made it clear that we were just friends. It did made me feel good to know that there was someone in theater besides my brother with whom I could stay in touch with.

I asked Carol if Daniel was still on stand-by with the National Guard and she said, "Yes, he's still on stand-by. Have you heard when you're leaving yet?" She started crying. I told her we wouldn't know until the last minute and asked her if everything was okay. I felt so bad because I knew she was having a hard time with the thought of her little sister being in harms way. It's like it wasn't supposed to happen to sisters. I just wanted to hug her. She couldn't believe that I wasn't scared. I felt as if God meant for me to do this. I don't know if you've ever had a "God driven feeling", but this is what I felt.

January 30th, we were informed that we were not going as planned because there were too many soldiers deploying and there wasn't enough room for us on the planes. There was other breaking news . . . some of our Marines in support of the Saudi and Qatari Armored Forces had faced Iraqi tanks and armored personnel carriers and repulsed them. The tragic news was that 11 Marines died in this conflict. It made all of us realize that imminent danger and death was what we would soon be facing. I prayed for their families because of the suffering I knew they were going through.

Strangely, I was more determined to get there and help in my small way.

We utilized our time wisely and went through preventive medical training. We saw a film advising us of the types of snakes, spiders, sand flies, and various diseases, which were in the region. We were handed "Rules for Behavior in Combat" and a "Troop Information Handbook" explaining Arab customs, language, the dos and don'ts, and the natural dangers from their country . . . such as venomous snakes and spiders. A lot of this information we had already received at Ft. Sam Houston, Texas, but I guess one could never have too much additional training. Although I had been raised in Arizona and did a lot of hunting, I never cared for snakes. I knew how dangerous they could be because I had come across a few in the desert.

We then went to town and bought last-minute items we thought we would need. We boxed up our belongings that wouldn't fit in our duffel bags and mailed it to our family members.

We were told to spray paint our duffel bags with large "red X's" meaning Red Cross. This way when the duffel bags were down loaded, it would be much easier for us to locate our bags and separate them from the military ones.

Thursday, January 31 we were still on hold. Our dog tags were issued to us and we had more pictures taken. We were advised that one of our teammates could not go because his passport had not come in yet. One of the gals was a Jew and could not go because if the Iraqi's captured her, she would probably be in more danger. Watching CNN on TV, the news stated that a transport plane had been shot down today and no names were provided yet. Chills went through my body hoping we didn't have any casualties.

We were then informed that if our sleeping bag was put inside our duffel bag, then we needed to take it out. It had to be tied "on top" of our rucksack, which we would be carrying on our back. A rucksack is like a hiker's bag that you carry on your back with shoulder straps. The reason for keeping the bare essentials with our rucksack was that if our duffel bags got lost, we would still have a way to survive. We also had to make sure that we had a change of uniform and our sleeping clothes in our rucksack. So, our duffel bags were emptied and re-stuffed again.

Next came the cleaning details. We weren't staying in a hotel; we were in the barracks and that meant we were responsible for cleaning it. We split the details, and on this day, I got to sweep the sidewalks and floors.

Friday, February 1, we were still waiting. We went through the gas mask instructions again. Some of the military gear issued to us was not put together, so we broke down our duffel bags again and gathered all of our gear in order. We then started learning how to put some of it together. I never thought a kevlar (a hard hat) could be such a pain putting together. There are so many clamps for the inside webbing and it had to align correctly.

Next, we put our web belt together which held the water jugs, first aid kit, and flashlight attached to it. They called this LBE gear, (load bearing equipment). We learned how to properly strap down and wear the gas mask on our side and how to have it quickly accessible for a fast easy reach.

The liaison was Sgt. Shirley. She demonstrated how we were to inject the needle into our chest or leg if we were exposed to chemical warfare. She emphasized how important it was to respect the shots because of how easily it could eject. She said that one young soldier had laid his head on his medical packet that held the shot, and it accidentally ejected and went into his skull killing him.

Since most of us were not familiar with military lingo, Sgt. Shirley decided to teach us a few acronyms. I had never heard of so many acronyms and abbreviations in my whole life! We weren't given any paperwork listing these acronyms, so we were going to have to memorize what we could. The rest we would learn the hard way.

We were told once again to plan on departing very early the next day. The way we kept getting delayed, I had just about decided that we would never leave Ft. Jackson.

I had clean up detail again, and this time I was given the chore of buffing the floors. The buffing equipment was pretty large and I thought I'd have it done in no time. It looked fairly easy. All you had to do was turn it on and let it do the work. As soon as I turned the buffer on it took off with me hanging onto it. I went clear across the other side of the room. Thank God no one was in the way. I had to find someone who would stand on the front end of it so it would be weighted down and not take off with me. It took a lot of muscles, which I didn't have, and a lot of time. They said some "General" was going to inspect our barracks the next morning and we had to make sure everything was spic and span. I thought I was lucky not having to clean the toilets and shower stalls, but after my experience with the buffer, I decided the toilets wouldn't be so bad after all.

That night we had dinner with Sgt. Shirley and the rest of the Red Cross crew. She was great. She got a kick out of working with us and had several laughs. She said she appreciated our positive attitudes and eagerness to learn. We asked her to teach us how to "march", and so, after eating she demonstrated it to us.

Saturday, February 2, 1991 we got up at 0500 hours because we had to have the barracks cleaned (again) for a final inspection. This time I got the toilet detail. As I was cleaning the toilets I couldn't help but wonder what type of toilets we were going to have in Saudi Arabia.

At 0730 hours we were marshaled out to the street to stand with approximately 200 soldiers while our barracks were being inspected. Upon passing inspection, we then gathered all duffel bags (two each) and our rucksacks and took them to the street where Ryder trucks were waiting to have them loaded.

Afterwards, we returned to the barracks to have a final inspection of our ID cards, Geneva card, travel papers, web gear, kevlar, gas mask, mop gear, flack vest (to protect against shrapnel or bullets), and travel bag. We tried to catch a nap because we knew it was going to be a long journey, but no one was able to sleep.

At 9:00 a.m. we gathered in formation and could see several groups of soldiers who were further ahead of us, also in formation. The soldiers marched on and were singing out their march songs. We followed, closely behind, singing our march songs. We were quite proud of ourselves for getting this far. The walk was quite a distance and by the time we got to our meeting point, the boots that were too big on me were already wearing sores on my feet. I "sucked it up and moved on", as the military says, and when we arrived at the same meeting place as the soldiers, we were told to march around and gather to the front of the formations.

We had to form in alpha order and inner mix with the soldiers in alpha order as they were loading onto the buses. The reason for this was if there was a terrorist, and a bus was blown up, all of the Red

Cross staff would not be blown up in one bus. This way, the training wouldn't be a total loss. I thought this was pretty smart, but it didn't give me a warm feeling.

There were a total of nine buses, and each could carry up to 50 people. I'm not going to say where we were headed, because it's too much information available for possible terrorists (since September 11, 2001 terrorist attack), but the trip was enlightening. Since we were inner mixed with the soldiers, the soldiers were eager to talk. Everyone was excited, and talking was a great stress reliever. Many soldiers were surprised to see Red Cross deploying with them. They were especially impressed when we told them that each of us had volunteered to go. One soldier asked if we were "crazy". A lot of them didn't understand our services or how it worked during emergency situations both in state, and in theater. Needless to say, from this point on everywhere the American Red Cross workers went we were always busy. It was a good thing we had water in our canteens, because of all the talking I was doing. Everyone seemed to be pumped up and ready to go get the job done and get back home.

Upon our arrival at our temporary destination, we helped unload the duffel bags from the buses. We grabbed our gear and gathered in a hangar with the rest of the soldiers, waiting for our plane to arrive. The local American Red Cross staff and volunteers were set up in the hangar, handing out comfort kits and refreshments. There were also letters for "any soldier" from local elementary and high school students, wanting a pen pal.

Then, our plane arrived. It was a commercial plane that had been hired by the government to take us. I now knew the travel to Germany was going to be a nice trip, for there had been a couple of soldiers telling me that if we rode on a military transport plane, we would probably get air sick.

At about 0230 hours with our duffel bags loaded, we boarded the plane and headed for New York. Here, rank had its privileges. Officers and equivalents got to sit in business class. It was interesting to look down the isle and see nothing but heads and guns popping up. The ammo was stored below so the guns were empty, but just seeing our soldiers there, in their military clothes with their guns ready to take action when given the command was an awesome feeling.

I remembered what my father had always said; "the military is the backbone of America."

I knew I was a noncombatant and I hated war and killing, but I also knew something had to be done to stop the killing and torture being conducted daily in Kuwait. Sad as it is, sometimes it takes war to stop war, as throughout the Bible it talks about the many wars Israel was faced with, along with other countries.

As I looked at these young soldiers, I could see my sons' faces. Most of them were 19 and 21 years. They were young adults, men and women, ready to die for oil and ready to liberate the Kuwaitis from the terrorists, Saddam Hussein and his military force.

Upon arrival in New York (we were not allowed to get off the plane) we quickly departed at approximately 0500 a.m. headed for Frankfurt, Germany which was an approximate nine hour flight. Several of the American Red Cross Emergency Services volunteers walked down the isles of the plane and talked to soldiers making sure they were aware that Red Cross was also being deployed and that if they had a crisis or needed to talk to a "nonmilitary" person, we were there.

I had my first case when a young private asked me how our emergency services worked. He said that his grandfather had a heart attack just before he left. He didn't know what to do. He said that he was sure his grandfather had the heart attack because he was worried about him. I asked this soldier where his father was, and he informed me that he never knew his father. His grandfather was the only father he ever knew. He and his mother had lived in Wyoming with his grandfather and grandmother most of his life, at his grandparent's home. I asked him if he had notified his First Sergeant or asked his family to call their local Red Cross and he said, "I told my sergeant and she said that a grandfather's illness doesn't matter. I don't know if my mother contacted the Red Cross. I don't think she knows to."

I then explained to him what—"In Loco Parentis"—means to the military and it sounded as if his grandfather could be considered a Loco Parentis parent. I grabbed an ink pen and a piece of paper and began work. I got his name, rank, ss#, unit address, and all of the information regarding his grandfather, their address, and what hospital he was in. The poor kid was so worried, and I couldn't blame him a bit. How can someone keep their mind on their mission when they're in the middle of a crisis back home? I assured him that once we landed in Germany, I would advise the Red Cross staff there to send a message back to the Red Cross Chapter where his grandfather was located and then to the unit where he had come from.

No one knew which unit or command any of us were going to be assigned to until we arrived in "theater" (Saudi Arabia). I assured him that his unit back home would be notified as to where he was assigned in theater and that verification would be provided with a doctor's statement as to how his grandfather was doing. They were also going to provide verified information as to whether his grandfather would be considered, "loco parentis (LP)" which means an immediate relative. He was relieved to know that Red Cross was going to be there in Saudi Arabia to follow up.

No one could sleep on the plane. Tension was high knowing that we had left America and our families. There was no going back.

When we arrived in Germany, we had a 1½ hour lay over. Here, we were allowed to get off the plane. We walked from where our plane was to a large "fest" tent where the USO and Red Cross were located. I was able to pass the information I had gathered about the soldier and his possible LP grandfather to a local Red Cross staff. They were going to send it out so the Red Cross Chapter in Wyoming could get the verification and send it to his old unit. His old unit in the states would provide his address in Saudi Arabia because once he arrived in theater, his 1SG would advise his old unit of his current address.

It was very cold in Germany and the coffee the USO provided tasted great. If someone wanted to shower, they were set up for it. No one did because we were all eager to get going and didn't want to waste any time. We just wanted to start counting down.

Televisions were set up so we could watch CNN and see what was going on in the Gulf region. Watching the scud attacks and scud alerts and knowing that we were going to be experiencing it soon ourselves was weighing heavily on our minds.

As I looked around, I couldn't help but wonder who wasn't going to return. Everyone was busy doing different things. Some people were playing video games, trying to pass time away. Some people were quiet and others talked up a storm.

We then re-boarded the plane and watched two movies while in flight. The first movie was "*Ghost*" it made me think that if I returned it might be as a ghost. It was sad and didn't help ease our feelings toward the thought of dying and our loved one finding someone else. We had been away from our families for a short period of time, but it seemed like an eternity. I also remembered when *Ghost* first came out, it was right after my husband had died. I cried my eyes out when I saw it. But it was such a good movie.

The other movie was "*The Hunt for Red October*". This was a great hit among the troops. It was a military movie where it made you realize that you have to "outsmart" the next guy. The soldiers were all yelling "kick their butt", etc. It was great. This made me realize how important it is to screen the types of movies people watch on the planes while deploying.

It was obvious that we were on a roller coaster ride, having ups and downs with our feelings. The not knowing what to expect was the scariest, but I had confidence in God and our United States.

I discovered in talking with one of the stewardess' on the plane, that they too were volunteers and had offered to fly over with us into the danger zone. It didn't dawn on me that they too were putting their life on the line. I had assumed that they were being paid, but so what? All of us were. She said the airline company did not force any of them to fly and that the pilots too had volunteered to fly us over. They had been doing this on a daily basis. It made me realize that there are a lot of brave people out there, willing to put their life on the line to take care of their country. All for the love of their countrymen and women.

Everyone's attitude seemed to be positive and morale was high. The soldier's sentiment was that this is what they had been training for, and they were ready for action. War. They couldn't wait to get there, get the job done, and go home. Our next destination was Saudi Arabia and we couldn't wait to get it over with and say, "Mission completed".

ARRIVAL IN SAUDI ARABIA

We arrived at King Fahd International Airport, in Saudi Arabia, at about 0900 hours their time. We were all exhausted because we hadn't slept on the plane. As we landed on the runway and came to a stop, we had to run from the plane to a gathering point just in case a scud alert was going off. Our forever companions from that point on were our gas mask, kevlar, and flack vests.

The pilot did not waste any time in taking off and quickly headed back to Germany. I couldn't blame him. As I watched the plane take off, I had thanked God for giving us a safe flight.

The one thing I kept checking for was my gas mask. It was obvious hanging there, but it sure felt good knowing it was just a reach away. I knew the training we had undergone for our gas mask was probably going to come in handy real soon.

We then gathered in formation in individual units. There were four flatbeds that drove up and they were all loaded with everyone's duffel bags. We realized that our duffel bags had been loaded onto the flatbeds too. We had to have the military stop and download the trucks to find our bags. It was a good thing that we had painted big red X's on the bottom of our duffel bags. This didn't make the military appreciate us any more, but it wasn't our fault that we had to stay back. We had to meet with Red Cross supervisors in order to get our assignments.

We then waited for 1½ hours. We had thought someone was supposed to be there to meet us and it seemed like forever before anyone showed up. While waiting, you couldn't help but look around and wonder what the country looked like. I had never been outside of America before, and I couldn't really see anything. There were lots of military stuff, and the dry, sandy colored flat land seemed to go forever. There was a breeze blowing and I could feel sand hitting my face. It was kind of strange being in a foreign country with scud alerts going off and not knowing where to run.

Finally, Red Cross personnel arrived to get us and we were then escorted to Al-Khobar Towers not far from the runway of the Saudi Airport in Dharan. These towers were like high-risers, approximately 50 of them. I was told that they were originally built by King Fahd for the Bedouins (which were Nomads) because King Fahd wanted them to quit roaming the desert. The Bedouins did not care to change their way of life and still, to this day, roam the desert herding their camels and sheep. This sounded very old fashioned, and I had wondered if I would ever see Bedouins in the desert.

The apartment I ended up in was pretty large. It was on the 4th floor and had five bedrooms and three bathrooms. There were no beds and there was no water except in the kitchen sink. Try to imagine having approximately 12 women in this apartment with water only in the kitchen. We had to borrow a bucket from the room next door in order to haul water into our bathrooms to flush the toilet and wash up. This was a drag, but little did I know how much I would soon miss it.

We had not been issued cots yet, but I didn't care. I was happy just having my duffel bag and knowing that I could lie down to get a bit of shuteye. I set my alarm for 0600 hours. Just as I nodded off to sleep an alarm started sounding. Then the PA system started announcing, 'S C U D L A U N C H' and a high screeching sound echoed throughout the area. Everyone jumped up and grabbed their gas masks. Some started putting on their MOPP gear (chemical) but I was too interested in seeing what was going on to mess with my MOPP gear. I put my gas mask on, and jumped to a window and looked out. At a far distance I could see remnants of what were "patriots" being sent off in our defense. The red and yellow streaks coming up from the ground going high into the pitch-black sky were beautiful, yet at the same time, scary. I couldn't help but wonder how this technology was so precise and quick. I thanked God that we had people manning the Patriots. I glanced at the time and it was about 2:15 am.

Next thing I knew the PA system said, 'A L L C L E A R'. This happened several times during the night, and one of the gals was so scared that she slept in her MOPP gear and gas mask all night. Actually, she was the smart one. She knew she could get some sleep by keeping the stuff on, instead of jumping up, and trying to find the stuff to put on each time the alarm would sound. I felt sorry for her though. She was literally shaking all over.

If it wasn't the scud alerts going off, it was the five-prayer sessions blaring on the speakers throughout the community every day for the Arabs to pray. The first one I remember went off at 0500 and I thought it was beautiful. I was impressed, realizing that I was actually in Saudi Arabia, listening to their prayers in their language on the PA system. I soon lost the thrill when I kept losing sleep.

February 5 (after no sleep from the night before) I went to the mess room for breakfast. The meat tasted kind of like liverwurst and the hard eggs were cold. I decided to have fries with ketchup, and put a huge amount of ketchup on my plate. When I tasted the ketchup, I realized instantly that it wasn't what I had expected. I couldn't figure out quite what it tasted like, and decided to eat the rest of fries without ketchup on them. The coffee was instant, and with the lack of sleep I had, anything with caffeine would work.

I then went to the PX (like a small convenience store) right across from where I was staying and everyone was surprised to see the American Red Cross. There were a lot of questions in regards to how our emergency message center worked. They were surprised to hear that we were actually going out to the field where the divisions were. I told one soldier how it was exciting yet scary when the Patriots went off and he told me that they call the Patriots, "Scud Busters".

The first Red Cross meeting was at 2:00 p.m. where Red Cross Managers were waiting to select which one of us from the new recruits were going to be chosen to go forward with them. They were sure glad to see us. Harry Smith chose Michelle and I to be on his team. He had another assistant station manager there by the name of Sally, but she was currently at 7th Corp. working the emergency Red Cross messages.

Harry seemed to be about 50 years of age and told us how he had been with the American Red Cross for well over 25 years. He had also served with the Red Cross in Vietnam. He was somewhat bald on top with a scarcity of black and gray hair for his side burns. He wore rather thick glasses and stood to be about 6'3". Harry seemed to be a gentle quiet guy with a soft-spoken voice.

Michelle was about 20 years old. Her mother had deployed two months earlier with the American Red Cross to Saudi and was assigned to the Air Force. Michelle's hair was mid length and very blonde. Her eyes were a sky blue color and she was of medium build. She had the cutest giggle and she seemed to care a lot for our fellow soldiers.

We were both told that we were going to Al Quaysumah in a couple of days to join First Armored Division (1AD), where we were going to pull different shifts.

We were then taken to 7th Corp. to work. I couldn't wait to get started working. We weren't there very long before Harry came over and said we had to "in-process".

We had just gone through this at Ft. Jackson, but we were told this was a different "in-processing". This was where they kept a roster of all those who came into Saudi and where they were located.

After doing the initial in-processing I then went out to find something for lunch and found a quick stand where I got a hamburger and ice cream. It was great. I then found the newsstands and telephone booth. I couldn't believe how many telephones were set up from AT & T. It was great being able to reach out and touch home so easily. The only problem was the long line at the booths and I patiently waited to call home. It took approximately one hour standing in the long lines, waiting to finally call out. I felt sorry for those soldiers who had driven a long distance just to get to the telephone, because then they had to wait for a long time just to make that call. Because of the long lines, and to allow equal time for people, we were all on a five-minute time limit.

I now understood what my brother Paul and my friend George were talking about when they said that they needed to get off the phone because their time was up.

I also discovered how it was easy to get disconnected because of transmission problems. I ended up spending part of my five minutes trying to call back. This didn't allow much time to talk, but it was still good being able to say, "I love you" or "I miss you." Just hearing your family's voice over the phone gave you a warm feeling and helped build morale. I didn't realize it at the time, but I was soon going to regret having phones so easily accessible.

Scuds became a familiar condition, which would continuously come in at different times. There were different levels and we knew that when the sirens went off, it was time to get serious.

On February 6, I had set my alarm for 0600 hours, but it went off at 0300 hours. Michelle and I were dressed and ready to go before we noticed the time difference. We visited for a while and then went out for breakfast and found a different mess hall. It was great! We had potatoes, gravy and meat. I just couldn't stomach the eggs anymore.

Word got out that people were suffering from salmonella poisoning. From then on, everyone was told to check and make sure their scrambled eggs were cooked all the way through before they ate them. I chose not to eat any. I noticed that the coffee tasted much better, or maybe I was just adjusting.

We met a Major who was kind enough to walk us around and show us where the mailroom was located and how to get back to our building. I sent off 10 letters and actually took a nap. At 1400 hrs (2 p.m.) Michelle and I went to another Red Cross meeting and were told that we were moving to building #320 close to 7th Corp. We were told that we were going to move into Sally's room. She was the other Red Cross staff who had been working there for approximately two weeks. Upon dragging one of my duffel bags up to our new quarters, I saw Sally's duffel bag and a chill went through my body. Dejavu!

For some reason, I had dreamed of that very room several years earlier and had forgotten about it. The dream I had was while my husband was still alive. It didn't make sense to me at the time, and I figured it was just a dumb dream. Now I was actually living it. I remembered seeing that duffel bag with her name on it. I realized that everything that had happened so far must have been a part of God's plan. I didn't know why, and I especially didn't know if seeing her name on that bag meant something was going to happen to her. All I knew was that I was going to keep my head up and pray for things to work out.

I then reported to work at Dahran Air Force Base working emergency communications where I finally got to meet Sally. Sally was another blonde. She was approximately 50 years of age, with very short straight hair. She was British and had the cutest uplifting personality. She had been a volunteer in Disaster Services for the American Red Cross for years, and decided to volunteer for this deployment. She was happily married with a devoted husband. She introduced me to the other Red Cross staff who were working there.

The next thing I knew I was hard at work. I was amazed at the amount of emergency messages coming in. We had to send interim messages back on all of them, because we didn't have an answer in 24 hrs and had to report something.

This was where I learned how to operate the military TAC phones and I found out just what a pain they can be. My brother Paul and George, my friend, had told me earlier about TAC phones, and now I was learning what they were all about. We, fortunately, had a "high priority" on the lines, which kept people from preempting us (cutting us off because they needed to make a call from where ever they were located). The workload was tremendous. Red Cross staff had been overloaded with work for a long time because they did not have staff in the fields helping them. All message deliveries were being passed via TAC phones because messages couldn't be sent anywhere else electronically until Red Cross staff were set up in the outlying areas. This proved to be a nightmare because units and people throughout theater were constantly moving and almost impossible to locate right away.

For instance, a National Guard Unit would come into theater and would be assigned to another unit, and then they would end up changing units without our knowledge. Units were changing and it was impossible to pass messages to so many divisions and branches of service without Red Cross staff in the field monitoring the movements of these units. Phones were disconnected because of moves, and once someone was contacted, it was like pulling teeth, trying to get a response.

The War, of course, was the priority for the military and its mission. Our mission was the humane side of it. Getting word to soldiers about emergency situations back home and trying to see if they were going to be given emergency leave so we could quickly respond back to the Red Cross who sent the message originally.

I was then told that we would be leaving within the next one to two days to join forces with 1AD. This Division was out of Ansbach, Germany and they were now at Camp Thompson, ready to go forward.

February 7, I called my sister, Carol, and told her that I was being assigned to 1AD and was going to be moving out in the desert somewhere. She was so worried and said how much she was praying for me and everyone else. I told her that once I found out my mailing address, that I would call her back and give it to her along with a military TAC phone number where my brothers could possibly reach me. Carol said that Daniel was still on standby with the National Guard and couldn't go visit family because he had to be ready to deploy at a moment's call. She said how much my little cockapoo, (dog) "Patches", missed me and would walk around with a sad face. At least I knew my animals were in good hands.

I called my son Don and he informed me that he was getting married the end of February and didn't want to wait until I returned, because no one knew how long that would be. I tried to get him to take more time because he hadn't given himself enough time to get to know her, but his mind was set.

It was disappointing to know that my son was going to get married and I couldn't be there.

After hanging up, I then wrote 20 more letters and put a little bit of sand in them to send back to the states. Sally came in a little later and said that our flight was delayed until the next day. It reminded me of how long it took us to get out of Ft. Jackson.

Later that evening, all three of us gals, Sally, Michelle and I sat around and chatted for several hours before falling asleep. Sally would call us, "love". "Love, do this, Love, do that." It was great and we could tell right off that we were already bonding.

February 8, at 0215 another scud alert went off. Everyone jumped up and grabbed their gas masks. Sally said for us not to worry because the siren didn't go off first. It said, "SCUD LAUNCH" then a siren went off, then a long whistle, and then it said "All clear." We were told that a scud had hit in Rijahd but there was no damage.

The three of us went out for breakfast and Sally asked me if I wanted a "spot" of creamer in my coffee. I loved listening to her because I had never met a British person before, much less heard them speak. I had watched British actors on television, but it wasn't the same as seeing and hearing it in person. It was uplifting and would put a smile on everyone's face anytime someone spoke to her.

We then repacked our duffel bags to get ready to leave again. I went to the PX (store) and bought some Desert Shield letterhead and was constantly talking to people about the American Red Cross and what our mission was. Our boss, Harry came around and introduced us to Smedley. Smedley was another member of our team and he was approximately the same age as Harry, 50 or so years. Smedley was tall, had gray hair, and seemed a bit serious. He too had served in Vietnam.

Harry asked if any of us (there were now five total) would volunteer to go forward because he, Smedley, and Sally were not packed yet. At this time Harry made me think of him as "Felix Unger" of *The Odd Couple* on television. He had stuff everywhere and felt comfortable in that type of a setting. I couldn't believe all of the crap he had accumulated.

Michelle and I volunteered to go forward so that we could locate a tent for our residence. We knew they'd be arriving the next day, and we were going to have everything set up. We were taken to the airport, which was close to Kobart Towers, and boarded a military plane. This was the first time we'd been on a military transport plane and the captain was afraid that we would get airsick. He gave us each a bag, just in case.

Riding on a military transport plane is a lot different than riding on a civilian plane. We had to sit in these straps that seemed to flop around and the noise was tremendous. Thank goodness it was a short flight.

Upon arriving at 1830 hours (6:30 p.m.) on a small airport runway close to KKMC (King Kalid Military City) we were quickly let off the plane. We had to lug all of our equipment and duffel bags off. No one was there to pick us up and we had no idea where we were going, nor who exactly was supposed to be there to meet us from IAD. Our only known destination was First Armored Division. Michelle stayed with our duffel bags and equipment while I went looking for a phone. It was getting quite cold, and we had not eaten since breakfast and I knew we were going to have to find some food pretty soon.

I found a "reception tent" but they didn't have a phone so they directed me to the medical tent. I tried for one hour to reach 7th Corp., with no success. They gave me MOREs to eat (Meals Operational Ready), which were canned chili beans. I took some to Michelle, because I knew she was hungry too. I was concerned about her getting cold and being there alone, but when I arrived, there she was in a desert camouflaged HumVee (truck) with a soldier who had the heater on keeping her warm.

I then returned to the medical tent and they were in the process of having a "mock medical evacuation". A LTC (Lieutenant Colonel) had heard about my problem and had made a few phone calls for me while I was gone. He was waiting for a return phone call when I came back. By now it was 2030 hours (8:30 p.m.) and while I was waiting, there was another soldier, SFC Hernandez, who was on a phone across from me, calling his headquarters. I overheard him say that the Red Cross personnel were not there and that he thought their plane had been canceled. I walked up to him and asked him if he was looking for us and he was surprised. He wasn't looking for us in military uniforms. He didn't quite know what to expect, but a uniform was not something he had in mind. He was told that we were to arrive at 2030 hours, not 1830 hours. I was relieved to meet him and by now it was very dark outside and we were in what they called "black out conditions". This meant—no lights—unless you used a flashlight with a red or blue lense or were inside a tent completely sealed off with no light shining through. All the tents had blue light bulbs. This lowered the possibility of any bright light getting out.

SFC Hernandez then drove us, (in pitch dark) to "tent city" (a military compound close by with lots of tents). Traveling by vehicle with no lights on made us somewhat nervous. Upon arrival at Tent City, we were told that there was no room for us. This made me think of Joseph and Mary in the Bible when they were told that there was no room at the Inn. I had a feeling of helplessness being in a place where you have no idea where to go, or what to do. At least in the States I knew I could always call for help, but here, every minute and every day was different.

Sgt. Hernandez then said we were going to KKMC where he knew there would be room. Now, driving on a dirt road . . . alone . . . in the dark . . . is somewhat scary. Sgt. Hernandez could tell we were some-what uneasy, and smiled and said, "Don't worry—I have my pistol here and I'll take care of you". We were beginning to wonder if he knew where he was going but he assured us that we had nothing to worry about. He had a GPS (global positioning system) in the truck that gives directions and he could find his way, anywhere, at any time in the dark.

My only concern at this point was that we were going to find a huge ditch or fall into a canyon somewhere and disappear, never to be found again. Remember, I'm from Arizona where there are all kinds of mountainous terrain, so it was easy to envision this.

Then, just before arriving at KKMC, Sgt. Hernandez gave us some pointers. "Do not look at the Saudi men or make any eye contact. Keep your head down and walk behind me. That's one of the customs in Saudi and the women always walk behind the men. I will converse with them if it's needed. Do not try to speak to them."

Upon arriving at KKMC (where the Saudi military men train), Sgt. Hernandez led us through the gymnasium where there were at least 60 Saudi men playing basketball. They were making funny sounds and next thing I knew a basketball hit me in the head. Michelle knew what had happened and said, "Oh, Shit!" We kept walking and didn't pay any attention to them, following closely behind Sgt. Hernandez as he had instructed. We finally got into an area where there were Americans and boy were we glad. We had to go back to the truck to get our stuff and had accompanying soldiers to help us.

After finally settling in, we were given walls, like what's in a cubicle for privacy. Michelle and I needed to go to the bathroom, so Sgt. Hernandez showed us where they were located and he kept watch for us. They were "co-ed" bathrooms, so he made sure no one walked in on us unexpectedly.

Sgt. Hernandez gave us the "all clear" signal so we went in and looked in all of the stalls, but couldn't find the toilets. It was rather strange. There were these tall stainless steel type stalls and they had a sitting bench in them. You could tell they were showers and there was a plastic hose that seemed to be attached lower down. I couldn't figure out what the hose was used for. There was a small hole in the middle of the floor, and I knew that it was for the water to drain into when you showered, but there was no toilet. Michelle and I both went from stall to stall looking for the toilets and finally went to Sgt. Hernandez asking him where they were. He started laughing. We both looked at each other quizzically, and followed him straight into the room and observed him going to one of the stalls. He opened the door, pointed at the hole, and said that we were looking at the toilet. There was nothing to sit on, no soap, and no toilet tissue.

Sgt. Hernandez politely explained that they didn't need toilet tissue. They used the small water hoses to wash themselves after they were through using the toilet. To use the toilet, you had to squat. He said that this was why you didn't shake their right hand, because that's the hand they used to wipe with.

Fortunately we had toilet tissue in our duffle bags and had to walk all the way back to our area, and unpack our duffle bag, just to find the toilet tissue.

Lock down was at 2320 hrs and lights went out at 2330 hrs. I was a bit nervous wondering what I had gotten myself into. It wasn't the danger of the scuds that bothered me. It was the unknown of things to come. I felt I had enough adventure for one day and quickly fell asleep knowing that we were surrounded with American soldiers who were well prepared for anything.

February 9, we had breakfast at 0700 hrs in a large building with a buffet style type of breakfast. It was great. We had eggs, yogurt, sugar-bran cereal and coffee. We then headed toward our destination–TAA (Tactical Assembly Area) at Camp Thompson. Sgt. Hernandez told us how fortunate we were to be arriving at the time we were, because Camp Thompson had all of the necessary conveniences, a hot kitchen, ATT was in walking distance, hot showers in wooden shower stalls, and the mail room was close by. He said that they had just moved from the ISA (Intermediate Staging Area) and they didn't have all of these conveniences there.

All I knew was that our destination was somewhere further than where we were . . . across the desert. And the desert just seemed to keep on going with nothing but flat ground covered with sand everywhere. Once in a while you would see a small sand dune.

I had envisioned that upon arriving at our destination of 1AD that we would see thousands of tents set up. Not so. Tent areas were set up sporadically throughout theater. I was told that this way, if we were attacked, we wouldn't stand a chance of losing everything in one place. Ummm, good idea I thought. I guess that's why we have military intelligence and guys who know what they're doing. I couldn't wait to start performing Red Cross duties.

One of the first things we had to do was "in-process" at G-1, PAC (Personnel Action Processing). I thought, WHAT? AGAIN? The reason for in-processing was so that 1AD would know all personnel, active duty and civilians, who are assigned to their division and if we were a casualty, we would be in their system for processing.

Michelle and I were then shown which tent had been assigned to us. We were informed that it was a GP medium. I decided to ask for a GP large, since I knew we had more Red Cross personnel arriving soon.

They looked at me and asked, "What did you say?"

"I'd like to request a GP large, if it's available, because of the rest of the staff due to arrive and for our equipment."

They got the biggest laugh and said they could tell we'd never been acquainted with military life before. Come to find out, GP mediums were the largest. I couldn't figure out why they called them "mediums" but that just showed how unknowledgeable I was with military terms. Once we were shown our tent, then we were issued a kerosene heater and a portable generator. We were also provided cots.

We were taken all around and shown where the JAG (legal) tent, the MASH unit (medical), COM center (communication center where we would be receiving and sending electronic messages), postal tent, kitchen and dining tents where we would sit and eat, MWR tent (morale welfare and recreation), and several others, including the Chaplain.

While speaking to the Chaplain, he asked us if we were going to "jump" with them to the front. I asked him what he meant by jumping. In my mind I pictured me bailing out of a plane with a rucksack on my back. He laughed and said it meant, "moving". I assured him that where they go, we would go. We then left with the Chaplain to talk about business, and when Michelle and I decided to head back to our tent, we noticed it was starting to get dark. We then realized that all of the tents looked the same. They're all the same size and same color. All green. All mediums. Most didn't have signs on the outside. We walked around and around and finally found an MP (military police) who laughed and took us back to the PAC (Personnel Action Company) whom we were going to be sharing a work tent with.

This was a lesson well learned. Always know how to get back to your tent.

After rediscovering our living tent we decided to put a Red Cross sign on the outside for easy identification. We then got as comfortable as we could in our new home and started getting hungry. The mess tents were right behind us, so we weren't worried about getting lost again. This was when we had our first experience having an MRE (meal ready to eat). They were in brown plastic individual packages and placed in large pots of hot water. We each selected a package and took it to a long wooden table (like a picnic table but much larger). I cut mine open and it was tuna. It was pre-packaged with a hard cookie, cocoa to drink, and plastic ware. Michelle had pork in a small freeze dried package, with crackers, Kool-Aid, and applesauce.

It didn't take me long to appreciate Tabasco sauce.

Upon leaving the mess hall, we then went back to our tent and found that three 5-gallon water jugs were left for us. A soldier was there waiting to explain to us that if we wanted water, we had to haul it ourselves. He showed us where the water buffalo was located (a truck with a water tank) and we then started hauling our water for our new home.

By now it was pitch dark outside and it was "black out" which meant no one could have lights on unless they were confined to their tent, which had only two blue lights it. A couple of times we had a soldier come to our tent and holler at us because he could see a pin light outside. When there was a tiny hole, we had to tape it shut. We didn't realize how far a tiny light hole would show in the dark and if a terrorist was lurking outside, he could find us. The lights inside the tent hung down about 3 feet from the top and provided just enough light for us to get around inside the tent.

Michelle and I both realized that it was time to go to the bathroom. We had seen the white wooden toilets (like outhouses) earlier in the afternoon somewhere behind our tent. We took our flashlights (with their red lenses) and quickly discovered that our flashlights provided a very small amount of light in order to get around. It was a bit scary to know you were out in the dark, with the possibility of scuds, and not knowing what exactly was out there, nor where you were going. We finally went to another tent and asked someone if they could direct us.

This was another lesson learned. Always find the toilets, and count the steps from where your tent is to where the toilets are.

The tent we were in was okay. It didn't have any holes in it and it had wooden floors.

We had a visitor come see us. His name was Chief Guillermo of PAC and he told us that a Red Cross spokes person must attend various meetings every day. These meetings would be held in the early morning and early evening and the General in the meetings would expect everyone to be there and to report problems and progress. It was here that we would gather information regarding unit movements. This is where we would find out new names of units coming in, and their unit phone number and where they were located in theater. This would help us in knowing where service members and civilians were located, by the name of their unit. The Chief was going to be working with us in the same tent, and he and Sgt. Hernandez were going to be sharing quarters with us when we arrived at our new destination.

Michelle and I had a long day and were totally exhausted. We had decided that since we were the first Red Cross to arrive with 1AD and that we were going to choose where we slept from that day forward. The first in is the first to choose. So, we both picked the back two corners of the tent. This way, we had two walls around us, instead of being out in the open.

As soon as we collapsed on our cots, we started talking about our first day in the field with the Army, and what an adventure we had already had. We knew we were in for more experiences and needed all the sleep we could get. Next thing we knew, we were fast asleep.

February 10 we had been awakened three different times during the early morning hours with three different female soldiers temporarily coming into our tent. They were all new arrivals, just like us. Since there were no other tents set up with room for them, they knew Red Cross would not turn them down. We talked awhile after they arrived and they were pretty scared of what was to come.

At 0530 hours everyone was ordered to stand to attention and we were all checked for gas masks, kevlar, flack vest, and NBC gear (Nuclear, biological and chemical gear) to make sure we were ready in case a

scud attack came into the compound. We were then informed that
there were no "hot" showers. They were all cold and it would be best to
try to shower in mid afternoon because maybe the water would be
warmed up a bit by the sun. I couldn't believe how cold it was. It got
hot during the day, but at night, it was super cold. People in the states
would watch TV and when they saw the temperature in Saudi, they
thought it was nice. They didn't realize that human bodies could not
adjust as quick as the temperature was fluctuating here. I then appreciated the cold weather clothing given to us at Ft. Jackson.

That's one thing we didn't have. A TV to watch CNN. I really
missed not being able to see that was going on. We had to completely
depend on what our family told us when we called home or what we
were told by the military.

I went to our first meeting at 0630 hours, which was usually directed by a General, followed by several officers and NCOs (noncom-
missioned officers). There were soldiers there, each reporting from their
respective units and brigades. (That was one thing I never did under-
stand-what a Brigade was, a Unit, a Battalion, a Garrison, etc.) The
information we gathered was tremendous. We were provided all unit
names and brigades with TAC phone numbers, names of 1SGs and
Company Commanders, so we could pass messages when they arrived.

At 1100 hours our boss, Harry arrived with Smedley and Sally. We now had five Red Cross staff and we were informed that another one was on her way. Her name was Ramona, and she was going to be my co-worker, working the same shift with me.

This was a big day for 1AD. They were having a big barbecue. Steak and hamburgers. The first they'd had in several weeks from what I was told and it was terrific. Little did I know that this barbecue was going to be the last one for some time and that MRE's were going to be my best friend.

I volunteered to work the night shift, from 7 p.m. to 7 a.m., seven days a week. Harry was working with the communication squad to get us on-line with our emergency communications headquarters, EMERCOM, so we could receive electronic emergency messages.

After getting on-line, we immediately started receiving emergency messages, which needed to be delivered. Red Cross at 7th Corp was relieved when we went on-line, because it lessened their workload somewhat. We made up binders for all units and TAC phone numbers that were under 1AD and we were now in business.

I found it interesting as to how many soldiers were in 1AD and I asked Sgt. Hernandez what posts they came from in the states. He said, "From Ansbach, Germany."

I was somewhat taken back when he told me that the United States has more than 250,000 military personnel in Germany. I never knew we had that many soldiers in Germany. I figured we had five thousand or so stationed there and that the rest of the soldiers were stationed in the states. I was absolutely amazed when I found out just how large our military is and how it is spread throughout the world. Many civilians have no idea as to the strength, nor the amount of military we have. Especially the locations. You could tell I had led a sheltered life and had no understanding of our armed forces. I'm sure there are thousands of people just like me in the states who never thought about it.

Later that afternoon our other Red Cross worker, Ramona, arrived. We quickly became Desert Storm sisters. We could tell early on that we were experiencing something that would stay with us all of our life.

Ramona was in her mid 40's with a beautiful tan that gave an appearance as though she were from Spain. She had an unusual slang, like as if she were from New Jersey, which she wasn't. It was nice being with someone who didn't have blonde hair. Her black hair was just short of her shoulders. She was a short, petite person. I'd say she was 5'2". She said her husband thought she was crazy volunteering to go to Desert Storm. She had been a disaster Chairman and volunteer for several years out of California. She said her home overlooked the ocean and she knew she was going to miss the water. This was certainly a big change for her. Her family and husband thought she was crazy to leave California to live in the desert with military people, especially with the chance of being killed. She said that something inside her told her she needed to do this. I could relate. We jumped right into work and soon were doing everything together.

Since I had volunteered for the graveyard shift earlier on, it meant that Ramona and I started off with no sleep the rest of the day until we got off of graveyard the following morning. The ladies, by pair, pulled the 12 hr shifts, and would no longer be able to spend much time together as a foursome, because of the 12 hr shifts.

The two Red Cross guys Harry (our Felix Unger) the big boss, and Smedley, (Harry's assistant), would take care of the manual labor stuff. Smedley made me think of "Radar" in the television series of *MASH*. He always thought of everything and seemed to always show up just at the time we needed him. The guys were quite good at heating up our MRE's and they kept the coffee going. There were continual meetings and lots of statistical reports required by our Headquarters, which Harry handled. If one of the gals needed some time off to do something, usually Smedley would fill in. When we received a huge amount of emergency messages, one of the guys would come over and help out. Smedley was always answering the phones for us, or hand copying the messages. There were no copy machines where we were located. Harry was constantly running around spreading the good will of the American Red Cross.

Ramona and I soon discovered what unusual fun it can be while living the Army life.

Most of the toilets were called, "four-holers". You didn't have to see the toilets to know they were there. You could smell them . . . especially when the sewage was being burned every day with diesel fuel. Some of the toilets didn't have locks and some of them were halfway netted so you could see if someone was on the commode, from their chest up. Toilet paper was a commodity, and I always took my own toilet paper. Ramona would guard the door while I took care of business, and vice versa.

There were times that Ramona would drive me crazy. We had all been warned to watch out for sand flies and various types of snakes. Whenever we would go to the bathroom at night, she would walk in shining the flashlight everywhere before settling down and taking care of business. I'll never forget the time she yelled as loud as she could and scared the crap out of me. I flung the door open, because I was guarding the door on the outside, and went running in. A couple of soldiers also came running. She thought she saw a snake, but come to find out, it was a huge rubber band that someone had left on the window ledge. Probably put there by a prankster. It wouldn't have surprised me a bit if it had been one of those soldiers who came running over, for they were laughing pretty darn hard.

Spirits were high at times—especially when they were around us, because they said we made them think of home. I guess because of how ignorant we were of military life. I don't really know.

I'll never forget when a postal Warrant Officer came into the PAC tent yelling for "Red Cross". He asked, "Is there a Barbara Evans here?"

I said, "Yes, I'm Barbara Evans."

Then all of a sudden he informed me that he was chewed out from his boss for not educating everyone in regards to "what" could be mailed and "what" couldn't. I didn't know what he was talking about.

He then asked me, "How many letters did you mail with sand in them?"

I cringed because then I knew what the problem was. He was right. No one had said anything to me about it, but I guess common sense should have told me better.

"About 20", I said.

"Well, I don't know how many got torn up in the machines as they were processing them, but your letters jammed everything up and caused a lot of work."

I couldn't have apologized enough to him. I'm sure my face turned as red as red can get and I never did that again.

Everywhere we went, our names were the same. Red Cross. No one ever called us by our first or last name. It was always, "Hey, Red Cross". We quickly learned one of the important assets in us being there. We were someone to talk to who wasn't military and they knew they could trust us. We loved talking to soldiers and listened to them share their stories or difficulties. We especially loved looking at family pictures, which everyone seemed to have in one of their many pockets in their uniform. That was one neat thing about our uniform, all of the pockets.

Ramona and I were working our first graveyard shift and messages were coming in sporadically, sometimes 30 at a time. We were working pretty hard trying to get the messages out to the units and at the same time, we would have soldiers stop by to talk. Our American Red Cross sign was on the outside of our work tent, next to the main road where vehicles constantly would pass by. It was amazing how many soldiers had on-going problems at home with a loved one which concerned them deeply, and that was the main reason we were there, to get answers for them so they wouldn't have to worry.

Once a worry was resolved, they were able to give full concentration to their mission.

So many of them had childcare problems back home. They were so relieved when we would send a message back to the states or Germany to find information for them, through Army Emergency Relief, Army Family Assistance, or the local American Red Cross Chapter or Station. All of these agencies helped families back home and were quick to respond to our contact. This helped resolve some of the soldiers' worries and issues.

Several people were concerned about their spouses not knowing how to pay bills or a wife in Germany being nine months pregnant and no family member there to help her. They were surprised when we would wire back and request assistance from support groups to make direct contact with their loved ones and respond to our message with information as to how they were helped.

There were many who would receive letters, or when they called home, were told that an uncle or brother was seriously ill and their family didn't know to go to the Red Cross where they were located. We would gather as much information as we could from the soldier, and then we would request information from the local chapter regarding their family member.

If we weren't busy with new emergency messages coming into our tent, then we were busy either sending responses back or establishing new cases with the soldiers who came to visit.

Sometimes if a soldier came by to just "visit" we would ask them to come back later when we weren't so busy.

The Chapters and Stations back home were just as busy as we were. The main problem was in "response" from us. Our National Headquarters expected a 24-hr response from us, which was totally unrealistic. It took that long just to get the message in and transcribed and called into the unit, if we could find them. Sometimes it would take 24 hours just to deliver a message because TAC phones were disconnected or the units had moved on. Then we had to go on a tracing campaign. The time difference also posed a problem.

Once a unit was found, the soldier was some times reassigned to another unit, or was more forward or in a complete different location, and they had to transfer the message there. Sometimes by helicopter.

When our TAC phones were down, which were often, we would then have to find a "Tack truck" which had communication equipment inside it. Sometimes we had to walk a long way to find one.

Once we made contact with the 1SG and passed the message, they would get word to the soldier and then respond back to us as to whether the soldier would be granted leave.

We were always being preempted on the TAC phone. We did not have a priority phone and were constantly getting cut off in the middle of a conversation. We didn't understand why 7th Corp had allowed a "priority" phone line for the Red Cross workers at their location, but we weren't allowed one where we were. We were told it was because there weren't enough priority lines. We sucked it up and dealt with it the best we could. Then, when we did talk on the phone, the static was so loud; it was almost impossible to hear the other party.

Sometimes when the COM squad was down, our messages had to be faxed to us-that is if we could find a fax machine. Usually the nearest fax machine available to us wasn't in walking distance, so we had to depend upon couriers since we didn't have a vehicle. We had access one time to a fax machine, but the sand quickly destroyed it.

The system used by the Communication Center to receive our messages from our EMERCOM branch in Washington, D.C. was an antiquated one, but it worked. We would "handwrite" our messages, which we needed to send out, and deliver them to the COM Center. The soldiers at the COM Center would then enter it manually into their system, which was on-line to our EMERCOM office.

We enjoyed the soldiers at the COM Center. They always kept a positive attitude and would scream when they saw us come into their tent because they knew we had a lot of work for them to do, especially when they had a heavy workload to begin with. Sometimes we would catch them napping during their breaks. They knew that the majority of our messages were a Priority, because of the seriousness in them. We on the other hand would scream when we saw them come into our tent with 30–40 emergency messages they had just received.

We had a typewriter, but it "gave up the ghost" because of all of the sand, which kept getting inside it.

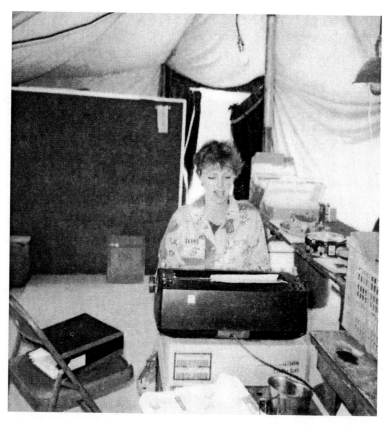

Cookie in mouth

Our mission was to find one way or another to get messages passed and get a response. It took a longer period of time than just 24 hrs. One of our largest nightmares was when we had messages for civilians or National Guard and Reservists. Many times new units or recruits would come in being attached to one unit or battalion, and then they would get reattached to a different unit without our knowledge. We also had small groups of service members from other branches of service attached to our Army units. We weren't aware of it until we received a message that we needed to deliver. Then we went on the search again. We had a few Air Force personnel working with some of our units and we had a couple of small "joint" task forces throughout our Division. Tracking took a lot of time and patience.

It was convenient having our workspace with the military Personnel, because they were the ones who would "cut the change of orders" for the soldiers departing on emergency leave. Most of the soldiers would have their leave orders changed by their local PAC and not come to the HQs PAC. This would upset the Hqs PAC, because it was difficult to control who was going where all of the time.

When they processed through our Hqs PAC we were able to immediately send back a message advising the Red Cross where their family was located, that they were returning. This helped us, because many times a soldier was sent home without us getting the message to send back home. 1SGs were very helpful, but since they weren't always with their soldier, it would take awhile to get word back to us from them as to when the soldier was leaving, or if she or he was leaving at all.

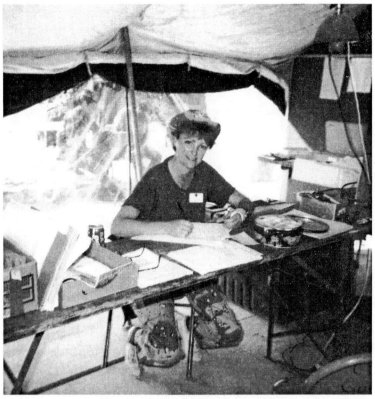

Soldiers in the backround given leave

We discovered that sometimes soldiers who processed through our area, had not been given the information in the Red Cross message. They were either told a small part of it, or they were told that they were going back home because of a Red Cross message, and didn't tell them why. One guy said he was given a copy of the message that his 1SG wrote down from when he transcribed it from us. He said that no one told him directly about his sister being killed in an auto accident. He was handed the written message and told he was being given emergency leave. No one was there to answer any questions or even talk to him about it. He was told to get his stuff and they loaded him onto the back of a truck and off he went. After a 6-hour drive from his unit, he finally arrived at our tent. He was having a difficult time holding it together, which was certainly understandable. He felt a little better when we talked to him, sharing the entire message. We cared and he knew it. We informed him that when he got to Germany, he could call the American Red Cross station, which was at the airport in Frankfurt, and they'd set up transportation to the states for him.

Units were everywhere, some as far away as 200 miles and the only method we had to communicate with them was by TAC phone.

One day, there was a Private who laughed at me when she saw my boots. I asked her what was so funny and she said it was the way they were tied. She kindly showed me how to tuck my laces in. I had them bow tied, and didn't think anything of it.

That's one thing we didn't learn, the dos and don't with military attire.

By now, my feet were really sore and Sgt. Hernandez told me that I needed to go to the medical clinic to get a "profile". I went to a MASH unit and they shook their head when I told them that I had new boots, but that they were too big for me. I had been told to "soak them in hot water" and I had walked around in them for one full day before leaving Ft. Jackson, S.C. I did what I had been instructed to do, but it didn't make my feet feel any better. In fact, I bought thick socks to take up some of the room.

The doctor told me that since I was a civilian, I didn't need a "profile" which meant the military medical profession agreed to a medical condition of the soldier. He told me not to wear the boots, and that I needed to get my tennis shoes back on. He gave me medication to start applying to the sores on my feet to prevent infection. The doctor said he pitied anyone who came over wearing new boots, especially when they were too big like mine. Putting tennis shoes on was the best thing I could have done for my feet.

Approximately February 14, Harry came in and advised us that we were going to "jump" to a new camp called "Log Base Echo". Ramona looked at Harry and said, "I'm not jumping out of anything!"

I cracked up laughing because I had been educated earlier as to what "jumping" meant, but she hadn't.

Harry said that we were to have our tent taken down and everything piled up high, ready to be loaded onto the trucks at 0300 hours.

We knew this meant two things. First, we knew we were getting closer to G day, (the day the ground war would start) and we were a bit unsettled thinking of it because we knew that some of us probably wouldn't be returning, but at the same time, we were excited that we were finally getting to the day of action.

Second, we knew our Communication Center was going to be down at least 24 hrs during this move. This meant our Red Cross station at 7th Corp Headquarters was going to have to handle our messages temporarily, until we were set up again. We had to notify EMERCOM to send our messages to ARC at 7th Corp.

There were all kinds of large military trucks sporadically located throughout the camp, loading all of the camps' tents and belongings. After everything was loaded, rows of trucks came in and we then piled into the back of the trucks. Getting into the trucks was a little awkward. There were no ladders to climb up on so you had to depend on some assistance from someone underneath giving you a great big shove so you could get up. It made me think of those big trucks in WWII movies showing soldiers sitting in them with their guns, waving to the news media as they went by. I thought it was going to be fun because Ramona and I got to ride on the end. Neither of us had ever ridden in the back of an Army truck, and we thought it was polite of everyone to let us sit by the tailgate.

Then, when we started down the road, all of a sudden dirt started rolling into the back and those sitting on the very end with the wonderful views also got the wonderful dirt in their face. Since we were now accustomed to sand storms and carried kerchiefs in our pocket at all times, I quickly pulled mine out and covered my face under my eyes. As I looked back at what used it be Camp Thompson, I was surprised to see how it looked as if we were never there.

Some time later, I heard a soldier say that we were nearing the Tapline Road (Trans Arabian Pipeline), better known as "suicide alley". As soon as we arrived on the road, everything seemed to come to a quick halt. We were now on a two-lane paved highway–which was jammed from as far as I could see, from one end to the other. There was nothing but convoys upon convoys and the Saudi people were driving around our convoys like maniacs. They didn't even care if another vehicle was coming. They drove like they owned the right of way and we'd better make room. I guess they did own it, but because of their attitude, it caused a lot of accidents. They drove as if they were on an eight-lane paved road like the autobahn (freeway) in Germany!

After surviving the timely Suicide Alley, we were back on dirt roads, making our way across the desert. As we were traveling, I heard a soldier say that we passed "Green 11" and I looked out to see if it was a golf course. It wasn't. There was nothing but sand and oh, how I had wished it would have been a golf course. I guess Green 11 had some meaning to the military, all I knew was that thinking of a golf course made me home sick.

After the long ride, we finally arrived at Log Base Echo, our final home before the ground war started, I was told that we were West of Kuwait, West of the Neutral Zone, and approximately 10 kilometers (one kilometer is approx. 5/8 a mile) from Iraq. 1AD was going to confront the elite forces of Iraq. Most of our armored division was located sporadically around Camp Garcia, which was approximately 2 kilometers from Iraq, or so I had been told. All I knew was that our Commander would laugh and say D-REAR (us and Headquarters) was at D-FRONT.

Soldiers downloaded everything from the trucks into great big heaps. It seemed like a lot of stuff disappeared. . . . our living tent to be exact. So, we ended up with another tent, which did not have any wooden floors and looked like it was as old as WWI. We ended up using MRE boxes for flooring, and it seemed to work out pretty well. Eventually, we were provided wood floors.

I noticed that the soil was different from Camp Thompson. In most areas it was like powder, where at Camp Thompson, it seemed to be more granular. All in all, it was still sand.

We were located close to DISCOM (distribution and supply center) and our work office was in the same tent as PAC, except this time, we had no chairs and the only thing we had for a desk was one long skinny piece of wood across boxes piled up for legs. We were able to locate some metal stands later. I asked one of the female soldiers in PAC where she thought some of our stuff could have disappeared to, and she said that if we didn't mark it and weren't there to claim it right away–Lord only knew who took it.

This was another lesson we learned: to keep a close eye on our supplies and everything else.

Now, instead of having our own TAC phone, we were going to have to share one TAC phone with PAC. Once again, there was no priority on the phone, which meant anyone with a priority phone could preempt us (hang us up while we're still on the phone). We tried to get another TAC phone, but there weren't any available. We knew this was going to be a real challenging way to try to communicate back and forth to the units. I had thought that we had it bad before having a TAC phone with no priority. . . . now we were going to have to share a phone. Just when you think it can't get worse, it does. I had decided from that point on, not to think that we had it bad, because there's always someone else worse off.

As we were trying to get reorganized from our recent jump from Camp Thompson to Log Base Echo, we had an Air Force pilot come into our tent asking to speak to the one in charge of the move. He was very upset. He said that one of the convoys did not have any markings on the top of their trucks and that when he was flying over them looking, he had thought we might be the enemy! It wasn't until he got to the last one in the convoy before he saw our markings. He came very close to firing at our convoy. You could tell he was upset knowing how close he came to shooting Americans and having to report it as casualties due to "friendly fire."

When he realized we were Red Cross, and that we were also in the convoy, he couldn't believe it. He said, "Oh my God, I could have killed Red Cross personnel also!" I don't know how the meeting went with this Air Force pilot and the Commander who was responsible, but I was sure glad he didn't fire on us. It made me realize that my guardian angel was still on duty in areas of danger that I wasn't aware of.

I'll never forget February 15 at Log Base Echo. All of us were on edge impatiently waiting for G day to start. It was as if the clock was ticking slowly and we couldn't wait for action. It was about 2:00 am and I was working graveyard shift. I took a break and went out and sat on a small desolate sand dune watching the world's greatest tanks, Abrams and Bradleys, quietly and slowly drift by undetected by those sleeping. All of our forces were finally coming together. They were headed for last minute preparations in Camp Garcia to begin the "mother of all wars."

I wondered how these tanks could be so quiet, and how many of these young soldiers were going to die. It's very frightening knowing you're on the brink of war and wondering if you will ever see your family or friends again.

Reality hit. We were here. We were at the starting line and things were ready to pop at any time. There was no going back.

At about 6:00 am, soldiers had gathered around camp and were filling bags with sand to make walls around the compound for protection against shrapnel and gunfire. It served as a protection wall for soldiers who would run outside to fire at the enemy, if they came into our area. War was more a reality. Each working tent was responsible for bagging their own sandbags. I helped the enlisted soldiers fill them. The enlisted soldiers told me not to because I was equivalent to a Major and that they were to do the work, but I helped any way. It was a nice break for me and helped me keep my mind off of things.

While working on the sandbags, a soldier came up to me and said he'd like to talk to me away from the rest of the soldiers. We walked around the back of our work tent and he expressed his anger towards our government for delaying us in going to war. He was fed up with having to clean his gun all the time and filling sandbags. I reminded him how we're all in this together and how we're all tired and ready to get on with it. I assured him that our Government knew what they were doing in delaying action. It was vital to make sure we had all of our necessary supplies, equipment, and soldiers, so that we could win this war. No sense in fighting if you're not prepared, right? I reminded him that his buddy next to him is depending on him being alert and ready for action and how much he knew "team work" was crucial. I told him how my life depended upon him, and I knew how important it was for all of us, more importantly his buddy, to know he was in a good frame of mind. He understood what I meant.

I could tell there was something else bothering him so I asked him, "Remember, we're all in this together but I can tell that something is wrong. There is something else going on, isn't there? Maybe I can help."

He explained how he had received a letter from his fiancée and she broke up with him. No wonder he wanted to get home!

I get so irritated with women and men who send "Dear John" or "Dear Jane" letters. Yes, it happens to women also. Many a person commits suicide for this very reason. It's almost impossible for a soldier to keep a positive mind when there are problems back home and when you're tired and beaten. The hot days, never being clean, MRE's, lack of hot showers, family still back home enjoying the good life while you might die any day. If a person needs to end a relationship, doing it by letter is the worst way of doing it. Especially when the tone of the letter is in a non-caring, attack mode. The best way would be to either wait until they return home or are out of a hostile situation.

Life in general isn't easy and learning how to cope in a difficult situation is just as hard. I didn't look for an "answer" for him, but I did converse with him about his other family members and how much they missed him and probably needed him.

I remembered the class we were taught at Fort Sam Houston about battle fatigue and stress. I asked him what he did for entertainment.

"Entertainment?" he asked. He seemed a little shocked that I asked him this, because this wasn't what he had expected. He was used to everyone telling him to suck it up and move on—so his expectation from me was somewhat redirected.

I discovered that he liked to jog, and I asked him to put the word out around camp that he was willing to start a jogging team open to anyone, to start at a time convenient for him. He laughed, and then started thinking about it seriously.

I later saw him and he was in much better spirits. In fact, he became a great support to us. He saw the equipment we were working with and found us a couple of chairs to sit on. It made him feel good to know he was able to help out a bit, and it certainly made us feel good too.

Word went around camp that as a "treat"; water was being delivered to the shower stalls for everyone. It wasn't heated, but that was okay. We were all tired of taking "spit bathes" or hiding out in our little corner washing from a small bowl. Ramona and I were one of the first ones to take a cold shower because we were off duty and it was late in the morning. Most everyone else worked day shift.

As we gathered our change of clothes and our shampoo and towel, we quickly walked to the showers. As we approached them, I remembered how many times I had walked by them wishing they had water in the tank which sat on top of each of them. They had been an ornament to look at for such a long time. Now, we were ready and we didn't care how cold the water was.

As we went into each of our stalls, a strong wind came up. Ramona's shower door flung open just as I had taken my top off, so I grabbed a towel putting it in front of me. As I ran outside I grabbed her door and closed it. She held it closed until I ran back to my stall and put my shirt back on. I then went back and held her door until she completed her shower. She then stood guard while I took a shower and somehow the water ran out. We knew we had to shut it off when we soaped up, in order to conserve what water was in the top tank for other people. We would then turn it on to rinse off. They must have been short of water when they filled the stalls, because it took no time at all for my shower stall to run out of water.

I kept thinking that maybe it was plugged or the showerhead somehow slipped off. As I looked at the showerhead, I would have to jump up approximately two feet in order to reach the lever to turn the water on. I would laugh at Ramona, because she would always bring a bowl with her to stand on in order to jump up and try to reach the lever. A person learned quickly that taking a shower in the beat up old wooden shower stalls was a "treat" in comparison to our having to bath in our private tents out of a small bowl filled with water. Sometimes we would heat our water on top of a kerosene heater, but it took forever.

While walking around our camp sight and saying "Hi" to everyone, a female soldier (quite a distance from where we were at) hollered at us, saying, "Hey Red Cross–What ya doing nosing around camp?"

Now I found it interesting how she could tell we were civilians, especially Red Cross. I had boots on that day (even with blisters). I was wearing BDU's (battle dress uniform). I had all of my military gear hooked on including my gas mask. My hair was short and well hidden. I just didn't get it. How on earth could she tell that I was a civilian, especially Red Cross? When I approached her, I asked her to educate me.

She said there was something about my walk that told her that I had not been wearing boots for long.

I then told her about my boots being new and wearing boulder size blisters on my feet. A couple of other gals came over and they all continued to laugh and tease us.

One gal pointed out that my dog tags were on the outside of my tee shirt. "So"??????? I asked. "I always wear a necklace on the outside so people can see it."

"But you're not supposed to in the military. It's supposed to be tucked underneath your tee shirt." They realized that I had not been through any training and quickly pointed out my earrings.

"Now What?" I asked. "What's wrong with my ear rings?"

"You're supposed to wear small ear rings which compliment the uniform, not large ones that are noticeable," they said.

"Well then, what's the point in wearing them if they're not going to be noticed?"

Again, they all got a chuckle and then again, pointed out another problem. "My pants were not "bloused right."

They showed me these green rubber band things and taught me how to "blouse" the bottom of the legs of my pants. The green rubber band things kept the strings from hanging down from my pants and made them look better. It also kept the bugs and spiders out.

One of the gals laughed and said, "We don't want you Red Crossers to be like us because that's what makes you "special," and not "military." It reminded them of "home".

One of the gals called us, "The calm of the storm", because we always put them at ease and tried to view things in a positive way. I got a chuckle when she told us our nickname.

We enjoyed our visit and ridicule, especially the laughs, even though they were making fun of us.

Shortly upon arriving at Log Base Echo, one of our fellow tent mates, who was a soldier, came up to me and said that if I can't walk in the dark without my flashlight, then I'm not a soldier. Well! That was a challenge. I knew terrorist attacks were a major concern and anyone walking around with a red flashlight was a prime target.

I decided to prove to him that I could walk around in the dark without assistance. So, the next night on graveyard, I decided to walk from my living tent to my work tent in the dark without the use of my flashlight. I didn't realize that a foxhole had been dug that afternoon while I was sleeping. When I started walking to my work tent, I felt pretty darn proud of myself because I knew I was going to prove him wrong.

Next thing I knew, I fell right into a foxhole. All I knew was that I was walking just fine and then all of a sudden the ground disappeared and I was in a hole feeling around while trying, at the same time, to figure out what had happened. I couldn't find my flashlight, but finally found my way out of the hole. I walked back to my living tent to see if someone could help me locate my flashlight and to see if I had lost anything else off of my uniform.

When I walked in Sgt. Hernandez asked me what had happened. He could see I was covered with dirt and everyone had a good time laughing, though I didn't think it was very funny at the time. After shaking off the dirt and washing my face, Sgt. Hernandez went with me and found my flashlight. No one let me live that night down and from then on, I was always told when a foxhole was dug in the area.

Sgt. Hernandez came up to me one afternoon and said, "Give me your hand".

I looked at him, knowing he was up to something, and asked him, "Why? What are you up to?"

He just laughed and said, "Come on, I want to show you something".

Sure enough, there had been another foxhole dug and he wanted to make sure I saw it.

One day it was just starting to get dark, and I was walking around, looking for a tack truck to make a few phone calls for new messages and to follow up on some other ones we'd not received word back on. A Major Clause quickly saluted me and then did an "about face" and hollered at me, "Soldier-come here!"

I then realized he was talking to me, so I turned around and went over to him.

He had noticed that I didn't bother saluting him back and thought something didn't quite look right. He eyed me over and then asked why I was wearing a uniform when I was the American Red Cross.

I told him, "It's not because I want to, but we have to follow orders from military headquarters in Washington D.C."

He was upset. He said that at a distance he didn't know whether he should salute or not, because of the square patch on our collar. I admitted to him that we'd had many soldiers salute us, and if we had the chance we would tell them we were civilians with the Red Cross. Soldiers would tell me, "when in doubt, salute." I would not salute back, because I was not a soldier, and I would usually "wave" and say "Hi."

Major Clause explained his concern. He speculated that if he thought I was a high-ranking officer, then a terrorist is going to think the same thing, making us a prime target. He felt our lives were being jeopardized and was genuinely concerned.

I said, "Major, I'm the little person here following orders. You know how that goes. I agree with you and would love to be in our own uniform, separate from the military uniform. I was also told that wearing civilian clothes would jeopardize my life and now you're telling me that by wearing this uniform, it is jeopardizing my life. It seems like I'm in a lose lose situation. All I know is that I'm not going to worry about it, but if you want to take it up line, that's fine with me. I'm just doing what I've been told to do."

He then loosened up a bit and asked me how we were doing and if we had good support. He realized we were there to do our mission, just like he was there for his.

I feel that soldiers should be the only ones wearing military uniforms for several reasons:

First, a soldier takes pride in their uniform and is taught the proper wearing of it. A civilian isn't taught this. They're given the uniform and told to wear it. Many of the civilians I saw wearing the uniform would have unkempt beards, long hair, or wear it like me-unknowingly inappropriately.

Second, a military uniform represents a combatant. When you belong to a Red Cross Society, you are neutral. I agree that there are times War cannot be avoided. I care for all soldiers, civilians and families, especially those who are in a war zone. That's why I volunteered to be here, in an area of danger to provide basic humanitarian service as a medium of communication for our soldiers and civilians attached to the military. I especially care about the proper treatment of all people, no matter where they are located or what the disaster is.

Our American Red Cross Society is committed to the Fundamental Principals of the International Red Cross: humanity, impartiality, neutrality, independence, voluntary service, unit, and universality. It seems to me that if I am captured while wearing a military uniform, yet proclaiming to be neutral, that our Red Cross society may have an impact on the ICRC (International Committee of the Red Cross) who are the ones allowed to visit POW's. If the ICRC is told that we were captured representing the American Red Cross, wearing a uniform, how could we be considered a noncombatant, and prove to be neutral?

No, we were not there under the auspice of the ICRC, but under our own national Red Cross society, which falls under the ICRC. I was willing to do whatever I was told, no matter what position it put me in, because I believed in my mission.

I also believe humanity is for everyone and it must be taught by each and every one of us to the best of our ability. This is the purpose of the Geneva Conventions. To protect the innocent and have rules of engagement. I know there are times it cannot be prevented. War is horrible, and combatants when put in a situation where there is no choice must do things. But it's when there are choices and someone, somewhere, has to believe that good morals and behavior must be the winner and override the opportunity to "get even."

Examples are the minefields, which are planted to destroy military forces, and are left to the demise of civilians. Usually innocent children and women who don't know anything about them are the victims. When the war is over, then these fields need to be cleaned up, before civilians are allowed back into the area. Many times civilians are allowed back, without having the land cleared. Many soldiers' lives are lost cleaning up these destructive devices. Have you ever been in an area where minefields are left purposely, knowing it's going to kill innocent children, and people who are not in the war? It's horrible and we Americans are so fortunate to not suffer from these atrocities.

Third, I believe that if it makes us a "target" by not wearing the uniform, so be it. We were ready to die for a cause, just like any soldier, news media reporter, or any one else. We were all there for a purpose and shared the same dangers, living and working conditions.

After returning from making follow-up calls on some of our emergency messages, I entered our work tent and was greeted with mail.

I had a letter from a friend of mine who said that she thought it was sad that I worked 7 days straight with no days off, she was happy to hear that I only worked 12 hour shifts, because that meant I still had time to get 8 hours of sleep and take care of what ever.

It was a good thing she wasn't standing close by because I felt like ringing her neck. Little did she know what was really involved, and I'm sure that most people in the states thought the same thing. They had no idea how much time and effort it took to get through one day.

When we weren't working in our work tent, we were constantly talking to soldiers. No matter where we went, we always ran into someone who wanted to talk and we enjoyed it. Even if we went to the toilets, we would see people. They loved having civilians to talk to instead of military people, and we knew how important it was to keep a positive attitude and a friendly smile, laughing about how things were. Keeping a positive attitude takes a lot of effort and energy.

When we weren't visiting with soldiers, we were in our living tent cleaning the dirt from the area, which had accumulated during the time we were gone. We had no Laundromat. The closest laundries were the two hands we possessed. Remember, we had to haul our water from water buffaloes in 5-gal jugs.

When it came to washing time, I would take a bottle of Dove soap and pour a bit into some water in a small plastic bowl. This is what I used to clean my BDU's in. Once washed, I would hang them out to dry and the air would blow sand all over them. It was a good thing my BDU's (battle dress uniforms) were the desert color, so the dirt blended in well.

Most of the soldiers in 1AD were wearing green uniforms. The ARMY didn't have enough desert uniforms to hand out and so First Armored Division ended up wearing their regular green ones.

I had wished that I had the green uniforms so I could match everyone else, but they had wished they had the desert. It seemed like the desert color covered up the dirt better than the green. Nothing stayed clean though.

It seemed like every other day we were hauling our water and of course the buffalo trucks were not close by our tent. Those 5-gal jugs are pretty darn heavy when they're filled. A lot of the times, we'd find that the tanks were empty. (tank trucks). Fortunately, we had plenty of drinking water in small bottles. Washing our hair and bathing out of small bowls always took a lot of time.

The only way we could heat anything was by using our kerosene heater. This process seemed to take forever. I remember trying to heat my MRE in a pan of water on the heater and I almost never thought it was going to get done. I soon learned to eat the MRE's cold and I doused the food with a lot of Tabasco sauce.

One soldier came into our work tent to visit us, because he saw our Red Cross sign on the tent. He was passing through and thought he'd say "Hi", because he'd not seen any civilians. He was surprised to discover that we did not have a kitchen (mess tent) in our camp. The kitchens went where they were needed the most at the front with the soldiers. This soldier said he was a "tank driver" and they would throw their MREs on the muffler, start the engine up, and in one second they would have a hot MRE.

Humph! I think that's the only advantage these guys had.

Every morning when I got up I would put a small cup of water on top of the kerosene heater so I could have warm water to wash my face. I would think about how fast it would be if a tank were here so I could go put my cup on its muffler.

No matter what you did, dirt would cover you. I had plastic bags and towels covering everything to try to keep the sand out. I kept my clothes and personal items inside baggies, but somehow, sand and dirt still got in them.

We'd zip our sleeping bags up to try to keep the bugs and sand out.

White underwear soon turned into a sandy brown color. I would do all of my washing inside our tent, in order to avoid getting dirt blown on them.

The shower curtains that were draped around my area in our co-ed tent afforded a lot of privacy especially for personal hygiene. Since we didn't have water in the shower stalls for showers, we ladies would put water in a small bowl and clean up the best we could. Taking care of our basic needs seemed to take forever.

We were fortunate to only have eight people living in our tent.

There were two Red Cross men, and four Red Cross women. We had an additional two men who were soldiers and worked in PAC, but lived with us.

We ladies strung sheets and rain gear all along the "half" mark, separating the men from the women. Fortunately, I had a corner by the door that afforded me two sides of the tent. We put a sign up saying, "knock before entering."

I remember the day I called my mother and when she asked me what I was living in and with whom, I told her I was living in a coed tent.

She asked me what that meant and after I told her, she got upset and couldn't believe that I would be living that way. Moms. Aren't they great? Actually, I never would have thought that I'd be sharing a tent with men either.

While trying to catch some sleep one day, I thought of when I used to go camping and how fortunate I was right now, (I kept telling myself) because I had a cot. When I first started camping, my sons were very small. I remembered putting our sleeping bags on the ground. So mentally, I told myself how I was "better off" right now than I had been before. The big difference was that "before" it was just a weekend of camping and fun–not a possible one-year assignment, but I kept trying to think of ways to appreciate how we were living. Such as, no dishes to clean, no rearranging the house, no bathrooms to clean, no beds to make up. The list could go on, but I'd stop because I'd then start getting home sick.

Many times, upon waking up, I'd look over at Ramona's cot and knew I'd have to wake her up to get her moving around. It always took her awhile to wake up and get ready to go to work. She said she hated having to get up and asked me to wake her if her alarm didn't go off. Sometimes I'd kick at her cot and hear her yell, "What?? What's going on? I was getting up!"

When I'd think it was her head at the end of the cot, sometimes it was either her butt, or her feet. She had a tendency to move around a lot on her cot, and she needed a lot of coffee to get going once she got up.

Sometimes I'd yell at her, "Ramona, get up!" She would moan and mumble a few words and start moving around, finally getting up.

One afternoon after waking up and going to the front where Harry and Smedley had coffee going, Harry and I started talking about Red Cross and his prior experiences. He had served in Vietnam along with Smedley, while working for the American Red Cross. They'd been around a long time and seen a lot of different kinds of living conditions. Harry said that he could honestly say that our living conditions were much worse here than in Vietnam. There were no sandstorms in Nam, they stayed in one location (living and working) and had hot meals three times a day. But they did have a lot of rain, and he didn't know which was worse, too much rain or solid sun and heat. There were a lot of amenities in their camp, including lots of recreation. Here, we hardly had any, but as he stated, "There's nothing that can be worse than the horrors and fighting conditions of the men and women who served in Vietnam. The living and working conditions may have been better for those who got to stay in camp, but not for the soldiers who left camp and fought. Also, the medical staff was constantly busy in Vietnam, unlike here right now, but, it will most likely all change in the near future."

Having had a brother and two brother-in-laws who served in Vietnam, it made me think of how fortunate we really were, because living conditions are not life threatening–you just have to learn how to tolerate it with a laugh.

For some reason, I couldn't laugh about one of the ominous living conditions, the toilets. Our living tent seemed to always end up by the toilets, which had to be burned every day with diesel fuel. The smell was staggering.

Sometimes I'd wake up to the lingering smell and decide that it was time to take a walk and get out of the area. We ladies would usually enter and leave the tent through the men's end. The guys could care less about us coming and going for they weren't into privacy like we were.

We were always accompanied by our gas masks, kevlar and flack vests. It felt as if it was a part of my "being".

Since we had constant possession of these items at all times, it meant that any time we changed, or had to go to the bathroom, then we had to remove all of this equipment, and put it all back on. We didn't complain about it though, because we knew that we might need it to save our life. I'd also look at the soldiers and realize that they had a weapon and ammo that they had to tote around; there was even a sign on the inside door of the "outhouse" reminding them to take their gun.

If we weren't concerned about chemical or scud attacks, we were in the middle of a sandstorm with tents going down. These sandstorms had two affects on people. One was that it was an additional workload, which pulled morale down. The other was just the opposite. There were soldiers who complained because there was nothing to do, so when tents came crashing down during a sandstorm, it gave them something to accomplish. It's amazing how life can be agonizing when you're bored with nothing to do.

Red Cross personnel always had something to do, especially at work when we would try to process emergency messages as soon as they came in. We would have to manually transcribe each message onto another sheet because the messages would sometimes come into us on a single sheet of paper, where we needed two copies. One was for our record, and the other one needed to go forward to the soldier's unit 1SG in order for the 1SG or Commander to be made aware of the situation and in order for them to notify the soldier. We no longer had a typewriter as it had quit working early on because of all the sand.

One day we had just received a typical 30 or so messages, and while we were in the middle of handling them, I overhead a Captain who was cussing. I stopped and looked at him. He was eating what looked like a small can of chili, and for some reason, every other word out of his mouth was a cuss word. It was as if it was his common way of conversing.

The soldiers in PAC were politely listening to him and trying to converse back, (being as he was an officer and they weren't) and they seemed to tolerate it rather well, but my momma always taught me that using the Lord's name is vain is the worst thing someone can do.

After hearing him go on for about 5 minutes, I just had to say something. I politely asked him, "How long has it been since your mother washed your mouth out with soap?"

He was stunned and the PAC enlisted soldiers looked at me and then quickly looked at him, not saying a word.

He looked at me and then asked, "You're not military are you?"

I then said, "No, I'm with the Red Cross and I would appreciate some manners."

He was at a loss for words, besides turning red. He became very apologetic and started asking if we needed anything, which he could possibly get his hands on. I asked him to take a couple of us to the AT&T phone tent whenever he had a chance since we had not been for several days and it was located several miles from where we were. He smiled and said that he'd see what he could do.

His name was Captain Bellows, and he told me that he was attached to 1AD to study biological chemicals, if any were found.

After leaving our work tent, he returned a few hours later saying he had to leave because he had received a call where his presence was needed right away. He said he'd be back as soon as he could to take us to the phone bank, and that he felt bad having to leave without living up to his promise. He promised he would be back. We figured it would be a few days, if any, before we'd see him again, because we knew there were more important things that needed to be done without him having to worry about taking Red Cross personnel to a phone tent.

It just so happened, that Captain Bellows returned to visit us a few days later when we were in the middle of a horrendous sandstorm. It was a bit chaotic and everyone was running around all over the place, until he started yelling out commands to the soldiers and brought some order to the mess.

Usually, when sandstorms hit, people would try to stay inside and hope that the storm would quickly pass by without collapsing your tent. Not this time.

Our tent on the women's end was collapsing, so I ran out into the sandstorm to try to tighten the ropes which had pulled loose. While out in the storm, I noticed the color in the wind. It was a smoky reddish color. It seemed as if I was in a maze full of red fog swirling around me filled with sand. Rain was beating down on me and the wind was very powerful. The tent ropes broke and I fell backwards, ending up with a sprung wrist. The other end of the tent held up. We were fortunate, because when I walked around looking at the damage in the camp, there were several other tents, which had completely collapsed. The morale tent was one of them.

I went back to our work tent laughing and said, "Hey, the morale tent is down, that's one heck of a way to build up morale, isn't it?" I kept laughing and eventually everyone else started laughing and told me I was crazy.

Captain Bellows said he had returned to take us to the phone bank, but because of the storm, none of us were able to go. We had too much of a mess to clean up. He said he was going to be gone for some time and hoped he'd get to see us again before the war started–but didn't know.

A couple of days later, we had yet another interesting experience. It was called, a "heat storm." Somehow, because of the heat and other climatic differences, lightening was striking around us, but there was no rain. I really wanted some rain because of how muggy it was, but then thought that if it did rain, then we might end up with water coming on top of us out of no where. Water has to run somewhere–and when you're on flat land–it still runs. I looked around the camp to see if we had a "wadi" (dry wash bed) but couldn't see one.

It made me think of Arizona and how when there's lightening, there's usually rain. Arizona is known for water rising quickly and the dangers if you're in its way. I quickly decided that maybe it was best that it was only a "heat storm" with no rain. I realized quickly how one minute you wish for something, and then the next minute, you wish for something else.

That's what the morale was like. Up and down like a roller coaster. We had been informed of a couple of soldiers committing suicide and we knew how important it was to watch for possible signs. Soldiers seemed to open up and listen to us easier than anyone else, and when we heard them complaining, we redirected their anger and fears to something more positive. It wasn't always easy. Sometimes just listening was the most important thing to do.

Colonel Forgahl, whom we worked under, told us several times how much he appreciated our hard work and especially our dedication to the soldiers and our mission. He knew how difficult the Army life was for us, and also knew that none of us had been acclimated to it, prior to our arriving there. It made us feel good to know we were appreciated and how he took pride in our work.

One day our boss, Harry, took a trip to 7th Corp. and left me in charge. One of the gals on the day shift crew had passed a message and made the decision to not pass the "whole" message due to the context. She was correct in doing this.

The American Red Cross guarantees confidentiality to the soldier and his family to the best of our ability. The way messages were being passed was out of our control. Very rarely would we ever get to speak directly to the soldier. Once a message was passed to the 1SG, then he in turn would pass it to the following person in command where the soldier was located. Usually, the messages were not protected and units would pass their handwritten notes "open" to other soldiers in order for them to take it with them and pass it on down.

In essence, there was no confidentiality and every Tom, Dick, and Harry had access to the messages. We absolutely hated not having direct contact, but there was no choice.

There was one soldier whose wife had been injured and the doctors were requesting his presence. She was hospitalized and needed him for emotional support, among other things. This information was released to the soldier's 1SG in order for his unit to decide whether to give him emergency leave. The rest of the information in the message was not what we felt would have any bearing in the determination of emergency leave, and was more personal and confidential. The problem encountered was that the 1SG found out there was additional information in the message that had not been shared with him. The 1SG found this out when the soldier called his wife while she was in the hospital, and she informed him how she was injured. When the soldier shared this information with his 1SG, the 1SG called me and wanted me to share all of the details in the message. I tried explaining to him that the rest of the message was confidential and could only be released to the soldier. If the soldier gave us permission to release the additional information, we would.

Next thing I knew, a LTC came into our tent and demanded me to provide him with all of the details. I told him if the soldier requested me to do it, I would do so, I tried explaining to him that we have confidentiality rules and sometimes must decide whether it's beneficial for the soldier, to release all information without his permission.

The LTC slammed his fist onto our skinny table and everything went flying. Everyone in the tent looked and you could have heard a pin drop. This was very embarrassing and the LTC proceeded to tell me, "You are here because of the military and you are to provide us with whatever information we request of you. It is the military that provides you the tent, food, and office necessities. Now I am 'ordering' you to provide me all of the information in that message, whether the soldier wants you to or not!"

I then said, "Sir, we are here because we are mandated through

Congress to perform these duties. I have an obligation to that soldier and if you read AR 930-5 it will tell you that any soldier is protected under the principle of confidentiality from the American Red Cross. This is an ARMY regulation sir, respecting confidentiality of the American Red Cross. I will be more than glad to provide you the rest of the information if the soldier gives me permission, but there are some things the military does not need to know. The fact is sir, his wife is in the hospital. The doctor is recommending presence due to her physical and emotional condition, and needs him there to take care of their children during this critical time. The rest of the information doesn't change things regarding his wife's condition and that's why presence is being requested. The soldier will get full details when he gets home, that is sir, if you are going to allow him to go home on emergency leave."

The LTC then requested my supervisor's name and phone number in Washington, and I provided him with it. He then left.

I called our National Headquarters to give them a "heads up" and they said I had their complete support. The LTC never called them. I went to my duffel bag looking for our Red Cross regulations and found them. I then took the original to his work tent. He wasn't there, so I left it for his review.

About six hours later the soldier whom the leave was requested for, showed up at our work tent on his way home on emergency leave. He was waiting for his orders to be cut and for transportation to take him to the next stop on his way home. I informed him that we would be sending a message back stating he was on his way. He thanked us for our support and helping him and his family

As a routine, we would always send a return message to the Red Cross in the states or Germany, advising them of the military decision. This way, they could tell the family members who were waiting to hear from the soldier what decision the military had made and whether the soldier was going home, or was going to call them. This would give them peace of mind knowing that the soldier had been contacted and what the pending action was.

Once we sent messages to advise if a soldier was granted leave or not, we always informed them that it could possibly take 2-3 days before they arrived at their final destination. People didn't realize that we were way out in the middle of the desert and it took a while to get from point A to point B to point C. They'd be brought in from their unit to PAC to have orders cut releasing them to go wherever, then they had to wait to be picked up and taken to another point, where they would be picked up again and taken to the nearest airport, which could be a day's journey. Then, after flying out, they would land in Germany, and have to deal with trying to get a flight out of there into the states. This all took time.

Before the ground War, the mission was demanding all of the time. It took a lot of energy, and quite honestly, the mission was the most important thing to the military. To defray from the mission because of a home situation, took a lot of time and a lot of extra effort, which they felt they did not have.

A lot of people think that there's always a wife left behind. Not so. There are many husbands left at home while their wives are deployed. Fathers were faced with raising children without their mothers. Then, there were single parents who had no parent to leave their children with and left their children in the care of friends. Some of these friends ended up with emergencies of their own or were put in a bad situation and couldn't continue taking care of them.

Try to imagine yourself being in a deployed hostile situation, in a land far away from home, and knowing there's nothing you can do when your childcare plan is breaking down. We would get a lot of phone calls from soldiers needing us to follow up on a bad situation back in the states and we would send messages asking for support from the support groups back home, or another family member or friend.

Deployments affect all people and all ages. Many families break up because they can't handle the stress of being away from each other and being the only one there who has to deal with problems.

So many of our messages dealt with psychological problem wives and children were having. Some wives eventually became sick thinking about their spouses dying and they didn't realize the impact they were having on their children. Children listen to everything. And when they see their parent crying, they get emotional. Children watch everything, and when they see their parent watching the television and constantly commenting about "daddy" being there, it causes problems. One of the most important thing families need to try to remember during deployments is the well being of children. Mentally and physically. I'm not saying that it's wrong to be concerned—but be careful not to express it and live it day by day in front of your children. Be supportive and find things to do. Get with other spouses, go volunteer somewhere; send neat things to your spouse and other people in the unit deployed. It's hard to be strong, but it's better for the person deployed to know you are strong and that you'll hang in there as much as they will. If you know of families having problems, go help them. Establish a support group if there isn't one, or establish your own support group in your neighborhood. There's a lot that can be done, but be careful of the impact of your children, because they watch what you are doing and behave the way you are. If you feel you have an emergency that is being ignored by the military and you've taken all the proper steps, you can always contact your Congressman. That is if you used Red Cross and other proper channels and nothing has worked.

Because of the time difference from the States, I handled most of the Red Cross Congressional's, which came to us from our Headquarters. They usually came late in the evening when Ramona and I were at work. Ramona gladly relinquished working them. This was where good record keeping came in handy, and that's one thing we prided ourselves in. As soon as we received an emergency message in, we wrote down the date and time it came into our possession. We then wrote down the unit phone number and the time we called the unit. We would write down the name of the person we made contact with. If we did not receive a return phone call in eight hours, advising us whether or not the soldier was given emergency leave; we'd call back again and follow up. The majority of the time, the 1SG wasn't in the local area of the soldier involved. They were assigned to him, but they could be attached elsewhere, in another location far away. Getting messages passed, decisions made, and the soldier notified took time. All action taken was recorded. That way, when a Congressional came in, we could prove, who, when, and how often we worked the message.

A lot of times, when we received a message from the States, we didn't have enough information for the military to make a decision. We'd then have to send a message back requesting additional information for the Commander. Then we'd have to wait for it to come back to us with the additional information and get it out as soon as possible. We didn't make decisions regarding emergency leave and a lot of people thought we did. Sometimes family thought it was our decision, but it never has been, nor never should be.

The majority of the messages were critical. Sometimes they'd come in with only 24–48 hrs for a soldier to return to the bedside of an immediate relative before they passed on. Once those messages came in, we knew there was no way possible for the soldier to get back that soon and our hearts were saddened because we knew the agony the soldier was going to be in. We would work as hard and as fast as we could, even though we had many obstacles. Poor lighting, lack of paper, phones going down, being disconnected and not being able to get reconnected, trying to locate tack trucks to call out, checking to see if there were any helicopters in the area, trying to locate fax machines when delivery of messages was impossible; poor office equipment which wasn't stable, and the list goes on. We also were not provided a vehicle where we could drive to different units to pass messages on. Delays were constant in getting messages delivered.

Military units were to pick up every day, but sometimes they wouldn't and we had to watch closely to make sure they were passed, one way or another. We would give copies of the messages to the Company Commanders at the daily meetings, but many unit COs were not there to pick up. If we located a helicopter, we would put the messages in a sealed envelope for the Commander to read. Some units would be without phones for a couple of days because of moves. We were totally at the discretion of the military and had to make do with what we had. That's not factoring in the hot weather conditions, sand storms, and monstrous flies.

Soon, D-REAR Command got involved and caused great "heat" from the command to the unit level if we had not received word in 24 hours regarding what decision had been made concerning emergency leave.

I remember another message that came in requesting a soldier's presence because his mother was diagnosed with carcinoma of her ovaries and she was going to undergo a radical hysterectomy. The prognosis would not be known until after surgery. When we followed up to find out if the soldier was given emergency leave, the Commander said, "There's no reason why this soldier should have to be home just because his mother is having a hysterectomy."

We reread the message to him and asked him if he understood what "carcinoma" meant. For some reason, when the message was taken in his unit, they did not transcribe the word, carcinoma. We were discovering that when messages were passed over the phone to the unit, sometimes part of the translation would be inadvertently left out. We had to follow up and make sure entire messages were shared, and shared correctly. We learned to have the soldier taking the message, read it back to us. This assured us that they had the entire message.

One day I was in the middle of talking to a Commander about the soldier's mother needing a hysterectomy and right in the middle of our conversation, all of a sudden a voice was saying, "Hi, this is Captain George and I'd like to speak to Barbara."

I said, "Hello. . . . I'm Barbara. . . . who did you say you were?"

He then started laughing about being able to preempt me in order for me to have the pleasure of talking to him. I knew he didn't realize the importance of our work or what was being done at the time, but I had to ask him not to preempt us anymore because we had very important calls which we didn't need to be preempted from. I asked him to call back, but he didn't. I felt rather bad about it, but my priority was in taking care of the soldiers and making sure the emergency messages were delivered and resolved.

I was able to reach the Commander by TAC phone again, and finished our conversation about the soldier's mother needing a hysterectomy and why the doctor was requesting presence.

One day a soldier walked into our tent upset because he had received a letter from his mother in Texas saying that his wife had left with their kids and that she told his mother that she wasn't coming back, even if the soldier returned. He had tried calling her once in awhile, but he rarely was able to get to a telephone. Then when he did, she was usually gone. He was upset and felt that it was an emergency since she left with the kids. He was ready to go AWOL (absent without leave) and go find his kids and hide them somewhere, where she wouldn't know where they were.

I walked outside the tent to converse with him about the paradox he would put himself in if he did what he said. He would be spending time in jail, not with his children. He would get a dishonorable discharge and it would ruin his career. I emphasized that it wouldn't be worth it and I asked him to go speak to the JAG office and directed him where their tent was. I also walked him to the Chaplain's tent because they were always helpful. I was sure that he would get some good advice from both of them.

As I walked back into the tent, I saw a scorpion on my shoe and almost died, right on the spot. After jumping around and yelling, "Oh my God, oh my God" and having a couple of soldiers come running over to see what was going on, they found where I had flipped it off and killed it. We had been taught to watch out for snakes, scorpions, and critters that bite, and I knew that a scorpion could put a hurting on you.

Sgt. Hernandez walked over and said, "Oh, it wouldn't hurt much anyway because it's a large one and large ones don't have much venom."

I said, "Quite honestly–that doesn't make me feel any better!"

He laughed.

One had to be careful in Saudi, because these critters were known to crawl into socks and shoes, so most everyone would keep their boots and shoes covered up when they were taken off.

Upon going to bed early the next morning after graveyard shift, I kept thinking about that scorpion. I snuggled deep into my sleeping bag and made sure it was zipped up all the way. I knew it was going to get hot during the day, but I felt I needed to be safe from critters. I was so tired and needed to get some good sleep. A few hours later, after tossing and turning and thinking about that darn scorpion, I finally fell asleep.

All of a sudden, I seemed to wake up and felt what I thought was a snake in my sleeping bag. I could feel something slowly move across my leg inside my bag. I slowly started unzipping the sleeping bag, and when I got it to the point to where I knew I could jump out . . . that's exactly what I did. I moved quickly, jumping out of my sleeping bag and knocked my cot over.

Ramona came running over, "What's wrong, what's wrong!?"

"There's a snake in my bag!" After slowly and carefully looking, we realized that the string that ties the sleeping bag up was somehow stuck in the zipper part and would move every time I moved. Talk about feeling stupid!

That evening a sandstorm hit and out came the scarves and the plastic goggles that were issued to me. I'd tuck the scarf just under the lower part of my goggles and then I'd let my scarf drop down around my mouth and chin, tucking it into the top of my shirt. This helped keep the sand out. Our tent didn't blow over this time, but we did get some rain.

The humidity was pretty horrid. It seemed as if it was 5 times worse right after a rain and the humidity caused people's body odor to increase substantially. I noticed that once a person stunk so badly, they seemed to become accustomed to the smell and couldn't smell them self. It was easy for people to "not clean up" because there was no water in the wooden shower stalls and it was easier to be lazy because of the pain it took to haul water in the 5-gallon jugs. The pain of cleaning up using a small bowl seemed to take so much energy, that some people were too tired to deal with it.

That's something my mother taught me growing up, and that was the importance of keeping one's personal hygiene clean, which keeps people healthier. I also knew that cleanliness helps keep morale up so all four of us gals would use my little corner (with the shower curtains) to clean up. Many times men and women would comment on how we smelled fresh. Though it was a pain to deal with, it sure felt good after cleaning up. One of the oils I used was Skin-So-Soft, Avon. It was a great hit and we were told that something in it keeps the critters away. I used it all the time.

I remember talking to a soldier who had come into our tent to pick up mail for his unit and he commented on how "we women" seemed to have much more time on our hands to clean up, since we were not allowed to drive into town. He actually resented having to do most of the driving, which surprised me. So many people were looking for things to do, besides clean their guns, and this guy was in here griping because he had to do most of the driving. I would have loved to have taken the truck for a spin.

Later, we were told that women could drive in camps, but not in the towns of the Saudi nationals. Then, a couple of months later, we were advised that if you're in a military uniform accompanied by other military men, then you could drive. We didn't have to worry about it, because we didn't have a vehicle. I felt sorry for the women nationals, knowing that they were not allowed to drive at all. It sure made me appreciate America.

Scuds were a real issue, even to us, way out in the field. We didn't have Patriots where we were, so we were told that our warning device for us if a scud was coming in, was a horn honking three times.

Another signal was to put your hands to your shoulders three times to warn others. That way people could see you from a far distance and know what you meant without your having to try to take your mask off and yell.

Because of the meaning of honking a horn and how it related to scuds, we were all told that honking a horn in theatre was a big NO NO.

A supply soldier drove up one day, in a big hurry, and forgot about the rules. He started honking his horn in an attempt to get someone out there to help him unload the truck. This caused everyone to start running. Needless to say, he was quickly educated as to his wrongdoing and probably never did that again.

Shortly after this experience, the ground seemed to shake and you could hear everyone start running. You knew something had happened. The way it felt, I thought a helicopter had crashed because of the sound and how the ground was shaking.

I ran outside to see if it were an accident and sure enough, it was about 200 yards from our work tent and dirt was shooting high into the sky. There were a lot of people running to the area, so I knew they were getting help. I couldn't help but think how sad it would be if someone died and families back home being told the tragic news.

Later, we were advised by our Commander that it was a scud that had hit.

A "dud" scud he said.

I was relieved to hear it wasn't a helicopter crash and then reality hit . . . I asked him, "So where were the patriots?"

"Well, they're in areas of more strategic value. I'm afraid that we would be just another number to write down as a casualty."

Needless to say, it gave me a strange feeling of danger and of being expendable.

While talking about the dangers, Chief told us that when things start "happening" (such as the ground war) and if there was gun fire, that we needed to high tail it out of there.

I told him that with my luck, I'd run right into the enemy, because I couldn't tell the North from the South and which direction would actually be safe. He laughed and said that you'd need to run in the direction away from the fire—but I told him that I appreciated his concern, but that I thought I'd stay put and suffer along with the rest of them. He just smiled at me.

I couldn't help but notice that while talking to the Chief, that these nasty aggressive flies kept buzzing into our faces while we were talking. These flies irritated me to death. I have never seen more aggressive flies than the flies in Saudi Arabia. When I was lying on my cot, I would look up and see all kinds of flies hanging on, riding the side of the tent as it moved when the wind blew. It was as if these flies knew we were there, invading their land and they wouldn't leave us alone until we left. Sometimes they would literally attack you. The flies in Arizona were a bit aggressive, but nothing like these flies. These were much larger and thoroughly loved irritating us Americans.

I think the one thing that made me the maddest was when a Captain who was stationed in our area, kept hanging around our tent. He had the audacity to mention "sex". Everyone had been told that sex was a no, no and a reason for discharge. This Captain guy (I never asked him his name) approached me one day out of the blue, and said, "You know the order regarding no sex? It is only talking about soldiers having sex with soldiers. Civilians can do whatever they want and with whom they want."

At first I was lost for words, because I didn't even know this guy, other than seeing him come into our tent and try to make chitty chat. None of us paid much attention to him. It made me so mad to think how he thought there was a slight possibility . . . and I had never given him any reason to think that.

I quickly replied, "An order for a soldier is the same as an order for me. Besides, I'm not interested " and I walked away.

Pregnancy was a real issue for soldiers. Some soldiers would purposely get pregnant so they could be sent back home. They didn't care if they left the military with a less than honorable discharge. They were scared and wanted to get out of Saudi before the ground war started. I remember talking to one gal who came into our tent and was going to be interrogated by the Army. She was telling me that the Army had been questioning her and wanted to know, "Who got you pregnant . . . because they're going to be discharged also." She openly talked to us about it. She knew we weren't military and wanted to "'talk". She said she honestly didn't know and didn't care because she was going home and that was her sole purpose.

I asked her if she understood the implications that not only would this stay with her for her whole life regarding her discharge, but most importantly she would have a baby to raise. She didn't seem concerned at the time. All she knew was that she was frightened of dying and knew that by getting pregnant, the military would have to return her to the states. The military did everything they could to discourage sex in the field, but when people are afraid for their life and they know this is an easy out, some will take it.

One evening I was out late, taking a walk around the camp for exercise, and was thinking about things to come. The war specifically. All of a sudden, I heard a noise coming from a wall where sandbags were filled. Now remember, this was during "black out" and my eyes had adjusted to the dark, allowing me to walk around. I also had my flashlight with a red lense, but had learned to walk around without using it. I could tell the noise was coming from two people. I cleared my throat and next thing I knew two people took off running. It's amazing what you can see in the dark when your eyes are adjusted. The guy was running holding onto his pants and kevlar and the gal ran the opposite direction with her shirt flying open as she was trying to button it. I laughed to myself because I knew they thought I was a soldier, possibly a military police who would arrest them. When I went back to my work tent, I was laughing and told everyone about it.

An officer happened to be visiting the PAC at the time, and the next thing I knew, an MP came in asking me where this had happened and if I knew who it was, which of course I had no idea. He seemed disappointed when I told him that I had no idea who it was and I explained to him where it had happened. He had wondered if it was outside camp, which it wasn't.

It was advisable not to leave the camp, because if you did, you had to know the password for the day in order for the MP's to let you back onto the compound. Sometimes I had to leave one compound in order to get to a tack truck to make a phone call. One day I forgot the password. This MP was determined not to let me back in. I gave him the password, but it was for the day before. I showed him my I.D. and he saw my Red Cross insignia, but he still would not let me back in. He had to call his Sergeant in order to get permission to allow me past him. He was doing his job, and I knew that, and I could have kicked myself for not remembering the password.

This was another one of those, "lessons learned".

One day after work, I returned to my living tent and started going through some of the personal items I had taken with me. I was looking for my clothes pens to clip some of my family's pictures up on the rope that was strung around my sleeping area. I was sure happy that I had taken a couple of sheets from the house to sleep on. I also had a small pillow with me.

I had a white teddy bear and he always seemed to be smiling at me every time I looked at him. My corner of the tent was my home sweet home and I knew it was going to be short lived, with my looking back a few years later laughing about it. (that is if I survived the war)

A person had to be creative in order to survive both mentally and physically. We used MORE cans for paper clips and what knots. We used the MRE boxes (which packaged several MREs) for drawers. We would take our plastic bowls with us and sit on them when we went to the morale tent to watch movies, because there were no chairs. Most of the time there were no movies or the VCR didn't work because of the sand. We used lantern wicks as tiebacks for the middle wall that separated the women from the men. The inside walls were actually like curtains made out of sheets and rain gear hanging on ropes. I always kept a couple of plastic forks in my pocket, because you never knew when you might be offered something to eat. I would also carry my large metal coffee mug with me and would keep it filled with coffee.

All of us developed a strong bond in both our working relationships and our tent living. We were all in this together. We knew each of us was going through the same experiences, day by day. There were times you'd think we were brothers and sisters, and I guess in a way we were.

After working my regular night shift, good ole Harry, as soon as he got up early in the morning would start his usual routine. He would turn the radio on, make coffee, and warm up an MRE and talk. Talk talk talk. I could handle the talking, but the radio blaring was too much to ask for. The girls on the other shift had complained to me about his rudeness in turning the radio on loud when they were trying to sleep, and I guess I had all I could take.

I yelled, "Harry, TURN THAT RADIO DOWN!" The talking came to an abrupt halt and the radio was turned down.

Later Sgt. Hernandez told me it was he who had turned it up and he apologized. I then felt like a heel, thinking it was Harry. I walked up to Harry and told him how sorry I was and he laughed, admitting that he was usually the culprit who would turn it up, but that morning, he didn't. He hadn't realized the impact it had on us.

Smedley was always writing to his wife and talking about her. She had the same name as me, Barbara. I had an extra teddy bear, and he was brown, wore BDU's with his dog tags hanging out over his military shirt. I gave it to Smedley and told him that when he hugged it, he could think of Barbara. He gave me that Southern, "Thank you" and said he was going to put it to use.

We shared all of our goodies we received in the mail. My sister Carol was great in mailing me canned beans, flour tortillas and canned salsa. I could live off of those alone, but would soon run out and go back to MRE's. People would talk about getting MORE's when they went into other camps, but for some reason, we usually did not get any. The further in the desert supplies were delivered, the more things would come up short.

Mail call was always important. The problem was, it took forever for the mail to catch up to us, and when it did, some mail got to us sooner than other mail. I'll never forget when a 1SG came in with his soldier, a Staff Sergeant. This Staff Sergeant was furious and demanded us to help him get back home because he had just received his first batch of mail. The first letter he opened, his wife told him, "It's nice having Fred around. He keeps my mind off of things and it's nice to snuggle with him. He seems to understand everything I'm going through. I've talked to him about you and how much I miss you. Watching CNN and the thought of your dying makes me break out crying.

Fred seems to know just when to come around." Then, she went on talking about the kids.

I asked to see the letter, and he said that he had torn it up and that's what he's going to do to this Fred guy when he gets back home.

He knew his wife had found someone else, because he was forced to leave her, only to sit here in Saudi, waiting, with nothing to do but sit in his tank while she found plenty to do. Something was happening at his home and he felt it was an emergency for him to return to kill someone.

I knew right off that we needed to get him to a phone, so I asked the 1SG to see what could be done in order to find transportation for him to get to an AT & T phone tent to call his wife.

It didn't make sense to me that someone would just blatantly write like that about someone else.

If he wasn't able to reach his wife, I told him that I could send a "health and welfare" message through Red Cross channels giving them a day and time that he would be at a phone where he could call and talk to her.

Two hours later he came into our tent all red faced and said he had to apologize. He had opened the first letter in the stack and didn't realize they were out of order. There was no date stamped on the outside of the letters for him to know which order to put them in before he read them.

I said, "Okay, so what is going on?"

He said, "I'm so embarrassed, I don't know how to say this. Then he started laughing while he stated, "Fred is a puppy and his wife told him about Fred in her earlier letters which he had not opened yet."

The 1SG didn't think it was so funny. He was concerned that his soldier was going to go AWOL and he was of no use to his fellow soldiers in the frame of mind he was in. The 1SG was glad that the War had not started yet.

I then ran to my tent to see if I had any mail. And I did. He was right. There was no date stamp on them and I had no idea, which one was mailed first.

Ramona was infuriated at her husband. I had received several letters, yet she hadn't received any. I kept reminding her that California is further to go than Arizona. She had actually talked about torturing her husband when she returned because of the lack of writing. Then, one day she received five letters and they were all old. She felt really bad, and cherished each and every word.

Next thing I knew, Ramona started mumbling that she was going to kick a friend of hers because of what her friend said in her letter. She had talked about going out for dinner, taking in a show, and going to bed after having a long hot bath. Not only did it make you miss home more, but it also made you want to break your friend's neck for sharing their wonderful experience.

Another fun thing about the mail was when you tried reading it at night. With "blackout" conditions, you had to read using your flashlight with either a red or blue lense. No matter how much it strained your eyes trying to read at night, it was worth it. I believe letters were the greatest morale boosters.

We had tremendous support from our Western Operations Headquarters out of California. They were constantly mailing games, food, snacks, books, and other things to us so we could use it or share it with others. We had so many letters that we didn't have time to write back, but we loved waiting to see what we'd get every day.

One day, a logistic truck drove up and was down loading boxes. Being a bit nosey, I went over to him to discover what he was downloading.

He said, "Mamm', I don't think you'll want any of this that I'm downloading."

"So how do you know? I've been learning how to utilize a lot of stuff around here". As I smiled at him.

"Well, okay. I'm downloading body bags. You know . . . what we will be putting the dead bodies in when the ground war starts". He grinned at me as I made a face and walked away.

It was a hard reminder of the facts that we were possibly going to die soon.

As I quickly walked away, I saw an infantry soldier cleaning his gun. I couldn't help but feel sorry for the infantry because they had to keep their guns cleaned continually because of the sand. I remembered speaking to a tank Commander earlier, when he told me how the sand was a major problem with them because anywhere there was oil on their tanks, there was a lot of sand clogging up stuff.

It was going to be interesting to see how well the tanks were going to advance once they got the go-ahead.

I kept walking back to my living tent and was thinking about the body bags and everything else and then all of a sudden I ran right into a rope which was strung across my normal walk path. I guess the good Lord had decided that I didn't need to worry about body bags and it certainly woke me up.

That's one thing you'd have to be careful with, and that was when you thought you knew your walk path, it could change day by day. There were tents everywhere. You would become relaxed, and walk confidently during the night toward your work tent because you were familiar with your surroundings, and then the next thing you knew you would trip across a new tent stake. Or you would hang yourself on ropes that were added from one tent to another during the day. Sometimes people would hang out additional ropes to hang their clothes on. Or people would reinforce their tents with additional ropes and stakes to prevent their tent from collapsing during a sandstorm. You'd always have to remember to be on guard.

Another thing I learned was that when I blow-dried my hair, I wasn't to do it at night. The generators we had would kick off when too much electricity was used. We only had two lights throughout our tent, but when I used my blow dryer, it would overload the generator.

Also, the generators were loud, but you soon got used to the noise. At first I couldn't sleep during the day because of the noise, but I soon found that if the generator wasn't running, I couldn't sleep because I had acclimated to it. I often wondered how I could hear the warning of a truck honking three times if a scud was coming in. It was almost impossible. I wondered if I would be able to sleep soundly again when I returned home without the noise of the generator. I couldn't wait to find out.

Just before G day, a new tent was placed next to our PAC tent in

Log Base Echo and it was soon filled with replacement soldiers. I asked Sgt. Hernandez what they meant by "replacement" and he said they were to go forward when the war started to replace those who were fallen. You'd think I'd learn to quit asking questions.

One replacement soldier was cleaning his gun when it accidentally went off, shooting through their tent and carried over through our work tent. It barely missed his head when it fired. It followed a path sending it high through the air at an angle. I heard it when it went off, but thought that it was a pop bottle being broken and then I wondered how it could be a pop bottle because we didn't have any bottles in theater. I quickly convinced myself that maybe one of the soldiers brought a bottle over with him. Next thing I knew, people were running into the replacement tent. The PAC Chief came over with several other soldiers and was looking for the bullet hole. It had traveled through our tent. Ramona and I just looked at each other. It was almost like we were in a dream.

There was another time a bullet went off because a soldier threw his gun down on his cot and had thought he cleared the chamber before he went into his tent. The bullet struck the soldier next to him in his leg. A MASH unit arrived shortly thereafter and took care of him. I was surprised to see how quickly the MASH unit arrived. They were great. They were all pumped up and ready for action.

As I watched the MASH unit drive off, I had commented about missing not being able to drive myself.

Sgt. Hernandez asked me if I wanted to drive a truck to the camp next to us, and I quickly said, "Yes, when?"

This was the only time I got to drive in Saudi Arabia. Ramona, me, and Sgt. Hernandez went together in a truck and as he dropped us both off, he told us the combination to the lock on the truck that we needed to drive back. He gave us the truck number and told us where it was located. Most trucks had a lock and chain on the steering wheel to prevent unwanted personnel from acquiring the trucks, because all of the trucks had the same matching key. In order to protect the unit's from loosing their trucks they kept them locked when not in use. As Ramona and I got into the truck we noticed that the chain went all the way down to the floorboard from the steering wheel and was welded. Unless you knew the combination to the lock, the chain stayed on the steering column and wasn't driveable. Or so they thought.

We realized that we had forgotten the combination. We used every combination similar to what we thought we had been told, but nothing worked. We knew we had about 5 miles to get to our compound and I realized that there was enough movement in the steering wheel to allow "half turns". I ended up driving around in half circles all the way back to camp. Ramona thought I was crazy but I was determined to get back to our camp because we were on a time frame, and needed to return with the truck. Being brought up in Arizona hunting and four-wheel driving, I looked at this as another challenge. My mother always told me, "When there's a will, there's a way." We made it back to camp safely and laughed all the way driving in half-circles.

We very rarely got away from our camp. Sometimes when soldiers were taken to the telephone booths, we'd get to ride along. I thought it was great having phones accessible for the soldiers, but we didn't look at it that way once we started receiving messages from the states from their family members, because of contact from the soldiers.

Telephone calls were expensive, and many times the soldiers would call collect from Saudi.. When the bills hit home a lot of families couldn't pay them. Some families were put in huge financial straits because of the unexpected enormous telephone bills. Many needed to get loans to pay for their phone bills and we would have to contact the service member to gain their approval for the loan. One of the phone bills in a message stated the balance was $2,500, because of calls from Saudi Arabia.

February the 23rd was the last day Saddam Hussein had to withdraw his force from Kuwait. He was given until noon and we knew things were ready to pop.

On this same day, I also thought about my oldest son, Don and his big wedding the following day. I hurt because I wanted to be home with him to share this special occasion. I was his only parent and my heart sunk thinking about how neither parent could be at this most special occasion. The only thing that kept me going was my mission and knowing that I wasn't the only one who was missing special moments to be with families. We were all in this together through thick and thin. Through good times and through bad times.

I could tell the ground war was going to start soon, for our forces had moved directly on the Iraq border and were ready to go forward any second, any minute. A couple of soldiers stopped by our work tent and asked us if our TAC phones were working because they had just come from the AT & T phone tent and none of them worked. We knew our TAC phones had been working earlier, but it had been quiet for a short time now, and we were enjoying the peace. We checked our phone and it was also dead. Harry came over from our living tent and told us that the radio was also out. We knew things were getting ready to pop.

Harry said, "They must be jamming all transmissions and that means there's probably a lot happening out in the desert right now." We all got real quiet thinking about what he had just said. I said a prayer and asked the Lord to please take care of our military. We also knew that the fighting could come our way. No one knew. We just knew that G Day had finally arrived.

G DAY—DESERT STORM. THE MOTHER OF ALL WARS

February 24, 1991 was the day our ground forces finally got their action. Desert Storm was now going to storm all over Iraq. We were now in "kick ass time" as a soldier had told me.

Finally the end to the waiting game was here, for good or bad. It was good to finally be at this point because it seemed like an eternity while we waited.

That afternoon a sandstorm kicked up but formations stayed together. We were told that 1AD was attacking the elite Republican Guards, the Special Forces of the Iraq army. These were the Madinahs Armored Division, Adnans Infantry Division, Tawakalnas Armored Division, and the Hamurabi Republican Guards Divisions.

February 25 an Iraqi scud missile hit the US barracks in Dhahran, Saudi Arabia, killing 28 U.S. soldiers.

February 26 the Iraqis fled Kuwait City.

February 27 coalition forces entered Kuwait City and 1AD, Iron

Soldiers fought in a battle on Medina Ridge against the Iraqi Republican Guard in Iraq. President Bush declares Kuwait liberated.

February 28 the cease-fire went into effect at 8 a.m.

March 2, the 24th Infantry Division fights the Hammurabi Division and it flees.

March 5th most POW's are released, but not all MIA's are accounted for.

All in all, a summary of the battle in *The Old Ironsides Special Issue* for Iron Soldiers of Desert Storm dated April 22, 1991, states the following:

> "Afterwards the human cost of the battle for 1AD were two soldiers killed in action during the fighting, two killed after the fight, and 52 wounded in action. The division drove deeper and faster into the enemy's rear areas than any other division-size force in the Kuwait Theater of Operations."
>
> According to the Army Times, they had destroyed a total of 418 enemy tanks, 447 armored personnel carriers, 116 artillery pieces, 1211 trucks and 110 air defense systems. They had captured 2,234 EPWs (enemy prisoners of war)."

In just four days–100 hours of constant movement, the "mother of all battles" had become, in Defense Secretary Dick Cheney's words, "the mother of all retreats." Saddam Hussein's fury was evident in at least 200 burnings of Kuwaiti oil wells.

I remember the stories that different soldiers would share with us upon their return, or the stories that the General Headquarters would share in their daily meetings. Several soldiers would comment to us about the dead bodies they saw and the smell. Some they had killed, but most were killed from the Air War and some of the bodies had been there for a long time. They had told me how the stench and smell is something that they'll never forget.

One soldier told me about not being able to trust any of the Iraqis. He said that his Company saw some of the guards coming forward with their hands held up high like they were giving up. They were carrying a white flag. This wasn't anything unusual because they had already taken in almost a thousand EPWs (enemy prisoners of war). When the American soldiers approached them, they were prepared to take them as EPWs, when all of a sudden; the Iraqis' dropped back behind fortifications and started shooting at them. Then, our soldiers took action and went in and got them out. Some were killed, but most were captured alive.

A few told me about how the tanks ran out of fuel and had to wait for the refueling trucks in order to continue advancing. They had never dreamt that they would advance as far and as quickly as they did.

Some soldiers talked about the enemy bunkers they came upon. Some of these bunkers were empty but hadn't been abandoned for long. Their food was fresh on top of plates. It looked like they had just sat down to eat. Some of the bunkers were still occupied and had to be forcibly taken.

A couple of soldiers stopped by to visit us and told me how there were more soldiers who died after the "cease fire" in a battle on the border of Turkey defending the Kurds than any other day.

There were a lot of unexploded ordinances everywhere. This claimed a lot of lives. NATO forces had dropped "cluster bombs" all over the place during the Air War. There were also mines planted in the ground that needed to be detonated.

Some soldiers including civilians lost their lives accidentally stepping on them. One civilian was in a jeep and saw "what he thought" was some type of shrapnel left over from the bombings. He had decided to pick it up and take it home as a souvenir. After placing this small item in the back of his jeep, he and his friend proceeded and hit a bump and it exploded, killing one civilian and injuring him.

There were many other casualties after the ground war mainly because of vehicle accidents sustained on the Tapline Road, or Suicide Alley.

If lives weren't lost because of accidents on the roads it was because of accidents from having a lot of equipment moving around where there were a lot of soldiers. Someone was bound to get hurt.

As soldiers would visit with us on their way through, a lot of them would complain on how upset they were because they had Saddam in their hands but couldn't do anything because they were ordered into a cease-fire. They were concerned that they would be deployed again to get him and wanted to take him out. I reminded them that our Government gave its word that once Kuwait was liberated, that we would stop. We were living up to our word. I also told them that just because you take out a bad leader, it doesn't mean that the next leader is going to be any better.

Shortly after the ground war started, we had a female soldier brought to our tent. She was heart broken and totally shaken up. Her fiancée had been killed during the war and she was taken to see him. They were now sending her back to her unit in Germany. She stayed in my living area because it was the only place she could have some privacy. The other Red Cross gals who were off duty were able to console her until her ride arrived.

I think one of the most devastating messages we received was from a spouse of a soldier who had heard that he had been killed in the war. She found out because of the easy access to AT&T.

The sad situation was that her husband was dead. He had a friend out of the same unit who knew about the incident, and as soon as he got to an AT & T phone, he called his wife in Germany and told her. He quite naturally was upset because it was his friend who had died and he wanted to share it with his family. He didn't mean any harm.

His wife, in turn, called the family of the deceased soldier to share her condolences, and the family knew nothing about it. The military had not had the chance to notify the NOK (next of kin).

Once our staff received the emergency message from the spouse of the soldier, asking us to verify his death, we had to confirm it with the Casualty Branch of the military. It was true. We had to wait until the family had been personally contacted by the military before we could send any information. Then, our national headquarters took over from there and sent confirmation to the local Red Cross Chapter in the wife's area so they could pay her a visit.

It made me realize how having phones so easily accessible can be so destructive, but on the other hand, it was one of the best moral boosters there was. I thought about how our soldiers in WWII must have had a difficult time with morale. Especially since they didn't have the benefit of being able to call home like we did. WWII lasted so long, and to think about how many of them were out in the freezing cold, on the move, and had very little contact with their family, other than through letters is saddening. It had to be so hard on everyone. We were so fortunate in many ways.

I was finally able to get to a telephone in mid March and called my mother. She had been worried sick since the news hit February 25 about the 28 people who died at Kobart Towers because of a scud. She remembered I had told her I was there, but she couldn't remember whether I had left. My sister told her I was in the desert, but my mother insisted that I was at Kobart Towers. Mom had been afraid this whole time that I was dead. I'm sure most wives, mothers and children were thinking the same thing about their loved one. I could sense her emotional strain while I was talking to her. She didn't realize the difficulty I had in getting to a telephone. It was a relief that I was able to finally call her and she kept crying. I couldn't help but think of the pain the family members of those 28 people who died at Kobart Towers were going through.

I visited a nearby MASH unit that had a few EPWs (enemy prisoner of war). One Republican Guard spoke English and told me that they knew the Americans were in Desert colored uniforms. They had been told that the green uniforms were the American's elite force and when they saw First Armored Division coming, they took off running because all of them were wearing "green" uniforms. I had to laugh. He was so serious. Little did he know that the Army ran out of the Desert type uniforms and so 1AD was stuck with their greens.

Now came the waiting game again.

The war was over and every soldier was ready to go home. But not Uncle Sam.

There were a lot of explosives that needed to be destroyed and all of the equipment that had been painted "desert" now had to be cleaned and painted "green" for their return. All equipment needed to be cleaned from top to bottom.

After that, the equipment had to be taken back to the port to be shipped back to Germany or left for further use by NATO.

One day a civilian friend of ours, Matt, who was a tank specialist and was there to see how well the tanks performed, asked me if I wanted to go into a small town called Hafir Al Batin with him. I couldn't wait to leave our compound. The war was over and now we had a chance to get out into the local community. Ramona and I did not hesitate to go.

While traveling into this small town, we came across a lot of people who were headed back to their home in Kuwait. Everyone was happy and giving us the "V" signs. Children including women were out and the whole town was happy. The women still kept their distance, but the men would go up and kiss the soldiers. I was able to buy some prayer rugs, a shawl, an abaya (a black robe that the women wore) and a borqoa (headdress for men).

We were later stopped on the road by a Saudi Officer who asked Matt to follow him to his home where he had Arabian racehorses.

Now I loved horses, and had two back home, so the thought of seeing horses was exiting. Matt said we needed to show respect by visiting, so we did. We got out and walked around petting all of the horses, and being a horse owner myself, I couldn't help but notice how malnourished they looked. One of the Saudi workers asked us if we wanted to take a horse for a ride.

Ramona said, "No-I've never been on one and I'm not going to now."

I said, "No, I can't because I have a sprung wrist." (It had been injured a few days earlier from a fall during a sandstorm).

Matt couldn't because he had a partial wooden leg, which he had lost during Vietnam.

Next thing we knew this Saudi officer was pretty upset with the Saudi worker and Matt went over to speak to him because he was afraid that it had something to do with us. Matt returned saying that the Saudi officer was insulted if we refused to ride and felt that his worker had done something to offend us. He was prepared to have his worker flogged. So, I went ahead and volunteered to ride and Ramona was helpful by taking pictures. Good friend! I rode around in circles and the Saudi officer and others came running out and took a lot of pictures. One of the Saudi men asked if I was Matt's woman and Matt said, "Yes, she is, in fact, they are both mine."

They offered to buy one of us from Matt, which fortunately for Matt and the Saudi men, they were told "no."

After I got off the horse, one of the Saudi men ran over to me and grabbed my hair and asked, "blonde?" And I said, "no, gray". He looked at me with a puzzled look and I quickly stood by Matt, asking him if he was ready to go, and gave him a look like I was ready to go right away!

We politely left and Matt said his goodbyes to the Saudi Officer. Everyone was happy. We knew we needed to get back before it got dark and before our next shift.

On the return, we came across some Bedouins who were herding sheep and goats. The women were in long black robes with shawls and scarves covering their head and face. They were standing behind all of the goats throwing rocks at them to keep them moving. Children were on burros and the Bedouin men were in long robes carrying staffs leading the flock. Some ways further we came across another area of Bedouins who were herding camels by driving behind them in their trucks. I was told that these were the "richer" Bedouins. One camp looked like they had just pitched their huge white tents and they were all standing out, watching our every move. Especially the women.

It was nice to finally have a break from work and see how these people lived. It was like living in Biblical times. It surprised me to see that nothing had changed in this country compared to what you read in the Bible.

Upon returning from this short visit and getting ready to pull our graveyard shift, I noticed my skin seemed to be covered with some type of a wet film. I had noticed that the air in the town was somewhat dingy and you could see what looked like black fog encircling the outskirts of the city. It then dawned on me about the oil wells that were burning. I couldn't help but think about all of the soldiers who were living in the area and breathing that stuff, 24 hrs a day. I had wondered to myself if any of our soldiers were going to get sick upon their return to their homes after this was all over with.

Matt later returned to our tent to present us with desert camou-flaged Bibles. He was happily married and proud of it. I really appreciated the men and women who loved their spouse and would show pictures and talk about them. Family has always been an important part of my life. I'm very close to my siblings and my sons and believe that a Christian life, especially in a marriage, is of utmost importance.

The "waiting to go home" for the soldiers was hard. We ran into problems when soldiers would call home and tell family members to get a hold of their local Red Cross and request their presence; they didn't care what the reason . . . even if they had to make something up. They were bored and knew they had a lot of catching up to do when they got home and they were ready to go home.

I had a few soldiers tell me this, and I told them not to waste their time, because unless it was a true emergency—and hopefully it wasn't—then no message would be sent from the states for them. I felt sorry for the doctors back home because they were dealing with spouses who missed their husbands and wanted their doctors to come up with a reason why they needed to go home.

Our workload did not decrease when the war was over. In fact, it continued at the same pace. We were constantly getting messages in. One message we received from a Red Cross Chapter stated, "The doctor requests presence because the wife is stressed.

We had to pass this message! The soldier did not get to go home.

Pranks were another thing that was alive and well. It certainly kept spirits high, or at least for those who pulled the pranks.

One day soldiers started coming into our tent asking, "Red Cross, where is the ticket we need to fill out for the drawing for the turkey?"

I'd look at them funny and Ramona asked, "Who on earth told you that?" And started laughing, looking towards me.

"Rumors are out all over camp that you guys are having a drawing and that we need to come to you to put our name in".

We got a big laugh out of it and the poor soldiers were somewhat embarrassed. I'd ask them, "Now just where do you think we'd get a turkey and more specifically, where do you think we would be keeping it? Do you also have plans on cooking it?"

He looked at me with a blank look and said he was going to kill someone as he quietly left the tent.

We had approximately 40 or so coming into our tent asking. It certainly gave us lots of laughs and made the soldiers who came into our tent feel like idiots.

I was so happy when the kitchen moved back to Log Base Echo. We started having two hot meals a day and one MRE. It was great. We no longer had to heat food up or eat it cold.

I was asked if I wanted to go on a bus trip to Kuwait to get souvenirs from vendors who were set up and possibly see some of the turmoil, which was left behind from the war. I declined, but said I'd like to go with someone the next day to get to a telephone tent to call home.

Three Red Cross personnel went and ended up seeing things they wish they'd never seen. When they returned, they were telling me about the dead bodies they saw and the destruction to Iraqi tanks and bunkers. They said the smell was horrendous. I was so glad I didn't go with them.

They also let me try on a Saudi dress they had bought. The dress was beautiful. They were telling me how many dresses they saw and how fancy the Saudi women would dress, even though we couldn't tell because they had to cover up wearing their long robes when they were out in public.

We were informed the first week in April that we were again going to "jump". This time we were jumping to a Town Center known as Camp Kasserine. It was built as a staging area for soldiers to come to, to wind down and get ready to be sent back to Germany in the forth-coming weeks. This was great news. We were finally getting close to the end, to going home.

TOWN CENTER—
CAMP KASSERINE

The day we jumped, nerves were still kind of touchy. All of our belongings were thrown into a big heap ready for the trucks to come and be loaded. Several of us were standing around talking and all of a sudden a loud "hissing" noise started and everyone scattered.

We soon discovered that it was a fire extinguisher that had fallen and was being sprayed. No one laughed because we knew we still weren't out of danger. Anything could happen and no one was going to be completely happy until we got back home and out of danger's path.

When we arrived at Camp Kasserine, it was absolutely wonderful. There was a huge fest tent with lots of recreation available, like pool, ping-pong, movies, card games, etc. They had plenty of hot showers with lots of heated water. There were mostly Pakistan's doing the cooking and we no longer had to struggle with MREs. We could finally plan on three meals a day and all we had to do was line up and get it.

There was soda pop that was cold. They weren't hot from sitting outside. Netting was everywhere with huge televisions and picnic tables were spread all around. Fest tents were set up with a variety of basketball courts, card tables, television, and video arcades.

Everyone was happy, and it was a major step to, "going home."

As I went around talking to everyone, all they could talk about was when they got home. Home. Soon. It was great sharing pictures of families. Families we would all be seeing soon.

There was a father and son who were in the same Division, but were in different Units. This was the first they'd seen each other since their deployment. It made me think of my brother, Paul, and I wondered where he was. He had not been able to call me, but I knew he was okay because the military would have advised my mother by now.

There were plenty of phones at Camp Kasserine, which were easily accessible and one could walk to them and make as many phone calls as they wanted.

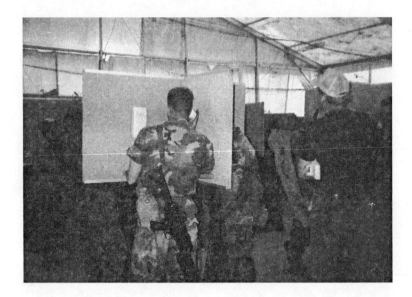

There was "near beer" which was non-alcoholic and was the nearest thing to beer. I was surprised as to how much it tasted like the real stuff.

Our living tent was great. We had newer tents and lots of lights. The first thing everyone wanted to do was to take a hot shower and call home.

For some reason our living tent was located by the wooden toilets again. There were urinals coming up from the ground with netting over them for a little privacy. As stated earlier, the girls and I lived at the far end of our tent and enjoyed what little bit of privacy we could have. Previously, we entered our tent through the front where the guys lived and left through the back, but not here. Our tent was so close to the urinals that we entered and exited from the front, so that we didn't have to walk by the urinals.

One night I had washed my clothes and forgot that the urinals were right behind us and I opened the back door flap and threw the water out. All of a sudden someone yelled and I then realized what I had done. Someone using the urinal was now "wet".

Sally started laughing at me as I put my hand over my mouth and flushed red.

Ramona and I seemed to have more time to see Sally and Michelle. Working 12-hour days and different shifts pretty well kept us apart. It was good being able to relax and get reacquainted.

I remember when I got my first "cold" Pepsi. It didn't settle well in my stomach because I had been used to drinking the soda pop warm. When that cold drink hit my belly, it really hurt, so I went back to drinking hot soda.

I couldn't wait to line up for the food. No more MRE's. After standing in a long line, and finally getting a plateful of food, I looked at my gravy and saw a huge bug in it. I went back to eating MREs.

A week later I tried eating from the kitchen again and found something else in my food. This time it was some type of hair in my salad. I couldn't tell what kind of hair it was, other than it was very coarse and kind of looked like camel hair.

I found out that MORE's were in the camp, so I decided to eat them and forget about the local food. I also went over to the Baskin & Robbins and McGunner (Army's version of McDonald's) and got a hamburger. The meat still didn't taste like a good ole American greasy hamburger patty, but it was better than nothing.

The 1AD band was finally able to get their instruments out and start practicing and playing. Their mission had changed and no longer did they have to worry about being prepared to do battle and the need to carry a gun. They now toted an instrument. They were great. We ended up having our tent next to the band members' tent, and the only time we got tired of hearing them practice was when we were trying to sleep.

We were still busy with performing our emergency communications and working our 12-hr days, 7 days a week. When we worked the graveyard shift, we couldn't sleep much in the day because we kept hearing the instruments playing right next to us. We still smiled knowing that it was the sweetest thing we could hear.

Also, the band soldiers were very considerate and helped us move our stuff. They even found a couple of extra chairs for us.

I asked one of the band soldiers where they found the chairs, and he said, "It was acquired maam . . . and you never ask how something is acquired." He had a sneaky grin on his face. I don't know which unit came up short, but we sure appreciated them and put the chairs to use.

There was a female Captain helicopter pilot who came to thank us for the support we provided her Unit while they were further out. I was amazed. I had heard of several females on the front lines when the battle started, and she confirmed it. I don't know where the news media got that the women were being kept in the back, because I knew for a fact that women in 1AD were also on the front lines.

I started calling home quite often. It was so good to hear my families' voice over the phone and how happy they were that I was soon returning. My sister asked me what the "noise" was that she could hear in the background while I was talking to her. The demolition crews were destroying explosives and I had become so used to the noise that

I didn't realize it could be heard over the telephone. This is when I found out that my youngest brother Daniel who had been on stand-by with the National Guard out of Arizona, did not come over. The war ended so quickly that he wasn't needed.

Another sandstorm hit while we were on duty and fortunately, the fest tent we were in held up without any difficulty. I found a paintbrush and started sweeping the sand off of our tables.

We soon got off work and then Ramona and I went to our living tent to see how well it held up. It was still standing and we were so relieved. We proceeded inside so we could clean up our living area and start packing, getting ready for our return back home, whenever that was going to be.

All of a sudden Ramona started screaming. I turned around and saw her on top of her cot pointing at a creature in the doorway. I soon realized it was a rat. It was the largest rat I had ever seen. I swear it was as big as a Volkswagen! It didn't run. It slowly walked into the tent and the more Ramona screamed, the closer it seemed to come. Then a Sergeant came knocking on the tent and entered because he had heard Ramona screaming. He slowly moved to the side because the rat had decided it had had enough and was now ready to leave. So it slowly walked back out.

I was on my cot by this time and was looking for my camera. Too late. It was gone. Ramona asked the Sergeant why he didn't do something about it. He told Ramona that he felt she was doing enough and laughed.

Ramona harassed the poor Sergeant and said, "You're a soldier— my protector. You're big and strong and carry a gun and you let a rat keep you from protecting us?!"

He laughed and we just looked at each other. That night neither of us slept very well, thinking that the rat was going to come back into our tent and bite us.

One of our neighbors was a Pakistan who was a barber. He asked me if I would write to him and be his friend. He mainly wanted to be able to come visit and set up a barbershop in Arizona. I politely told him that I would love to write to him, but that I couldn't help him with anything else. He was very disappointed, and I felt sorry for him because I knew how important it was for him to be able to come to America.

The PAC Commander informed us that he had put all six of us Red Cross personnel in for a Bronze Star for meritorious reasons. We were the only Red Cross personnel who received this honor not because the others didn't deserve it, but because our Commander saw what we did and took great pride in our work. He knew the obstacles we had to overcome and he also knew we were not military, but hung in there any way without crying about it. He said that with us knowing we were on the front lines, we still stood ready to do what ever it took to complete our mission. None of us cried . . . wanting to go home.

He stated he knew of soldiers who "broke" because of how a scud came close to their tent, and that he noticed that none of us let it hold us back or cause any emotional problems when a scud hit close by. He also said that even though we knew that two bullets had been fired at two separate incidents, with one bullet racing through our work tent, that we still stood fast and continued with our duties. He made us feel very proud.

We each also received a Scroll of Appreciation from VII Corps signed by Lt. General Franks which says the way it really was, "Scroll of Appreciation is awarded to Ms. Barbara Evans for distinguished service from February 1991 through May 1991 while serving as an Assistant American Red Cross Station Manager in support of 1st Armored Division, VII Corps during operations Desert Storm. Ms. Evans provided exemplary social services that focused on rapid communications and short-term crisis counseling for soldiers with personal and family problems. Overcoming a lack of consistent, reliable telephonic and electronic communications, she succeeded in passing messages to and from soldiers and their families. Her exceptional performance of duty reflects great credit upon her, VII Corps, and the American Red Cross." I had never heard of civilians receiving awards, and this was absolutely wonderful.

We had several visitors come through to see the Town Center and say "hi and thanks" to the American Red Cross. Some were Lt. General John J. Yeosock, commander of all Army forces in Southwest Asia, Lt. General Frederick Franks, commander, VII Corps; Major General Ronald Griffith, commander, 1st Armored Division; and CSM Richard Cayton, 1st Armored Division.

MISSION COMPLETED, TIME TO GO HOME

Approximately April 22nd we finally moved to King Khalid Military City so we could close out our station. Most of the 1AD soldiers had returned home. Upon arriving at KKMC we again were in a Saudi compound with the Saudi Army all around us.

When we walked from our living quarters to work late at night, we had an MP go with us to avoid any mishappenings. He told us that there had been a female soldier attacked from some local nationals while she was out jogging early in the morning. The Saudi culture did not allow women to mix with men and they did not have much respect for women who lived and went to war with the men. Especially if a woman was out running around by herself early in the morning or late at night. Culture differences are known to cause problems sometimes, and there were a few times it certainly did. I was told that this American female soldier was attacked right in front of the complex where our Special Forces were staying. In no time were some of our Special Forces out there educating the Saudis in the worst way. Some Saudi's were hospitalized during this struggle and it almost turned into an international incident. It caused a lot of changes to the way things were being conducted by our American forces.

The building we lived in was a coed building. Our room consisted of about six beds where females boarded. Men were across the hall in other rooms.

The bathrooms were again coed, but this time I wasn't surprised about where the toilets were located–in the shower stall and a hole in the floor. The shower stalls inside the buildings had a metal type of siding and were very tall eliminating any looky loos. They were totally enclosed which provided complete privacy to the person who was inside. I would change my clothes inside the shower stalls and come out and brush my teeth at the sink. There were several sinks all in a row and since the bathrooms were coed, you would have men and women coming out of their shower stalls walking up to the sinks.

I was in the middle of blow-drying my hair and couldn't help but notice a dripping wet soldier who came out with his towel wrapped around him. He walked up to the sink next to me to shave. I couldn't take it any longer. I grabbed my stuff and went to my room and finished putting my makeup on.

The only time I'd been around a dripping wet man with only a towel on was with my husband. The other gals laughed at me.

In a way I missed the way we had been living in our tents. It was rough, and I knew it was over. We had wanted everything to be over with for so long, and now that it finally got here, I had a feeling of emptiness and knew this Chapter in each of our lives was over. There was no going back–just memories. Some good, some bad.

April 27, Michelle, Sally and Smedley got to go home first. Actually we were asked, and Ramona and I said we'd love to stay back and close up. Ramona decided that when we both left, that she was going to have a stop over in Europe and visit friends. I on the other hand was going to head straight home. Harry stayed back, since he was the Station Manager responsible for closing out 1AD. It was sad, because we knew we'd never be together like this again.

April 29, Ramona and I headed home. I was taken to the Airport and stayed in a fest tent, sleeping on a cot where there were hundreds of other soldiers. Ramona went on to another departing area and was going to catch a military hop to Italy.

April 30 at 0500 hrs I had a customs inspection of my duffel bags. All of my stuff was dumped out onto cots for everyone to see. There were dogs going around and sniffing. I had a soldier ask me about a couple of books I had, which had been given to me from an American soldier. They were taken out of the bunkers of the Iraqi military. They were training manuals with lots of pictures, including good ole Saddaam himself. He looked at them and gave me the go ahead to take them with me.

Once we passed the inspection we re-packed our duffel bags and then carried them out to the road to have them loaded onto flat bed trucks, which were going to take them to the planes and load them. We waited under camo netting by the dirt road for approximately 8 hours and then at 1435 hrs we loaded onto buses and arrived at other tents with TVs. There, we went through inspections of our carry ons and were given boarding passes. At 1730 hrs we loaded onto buses again. Nonsmokers vs. smokers and we were on our way to the terminal. We finally boarded the planes and the first thing soldiers' starting asking was, "Where's the booze? We want to order a drink."

The flight attendant had to explain that alcohol was not allowed on flights any more.

Some of the soldiers became very angry and finally a Colonel stood up and called attention and informed them that because of the state of previous soldiers arriving at their home base "drunk" and upsetting family members and the military, that the ARMY commanding General ordered, "No booze on the flights."

After moaning and groaning and everyone settling in, we were then informed that we were going to Rome first. Everyone was happy and couldn't wait until we finally touched ground where family was. Upon arriving in Rome, we had to stay 2-½ hrs on the plane to refuel. No one was allowed off and soon we were on our way to Germany.

May 1 at 0400 hrs we landed in Frankfurt, Germany at Rhein Mein Airport. We boarded a shuttle bus that took us to the USO where we waited for our duffel bags to arrive. I then realized that everyone on the plane was stationed in Germany and they had loaded all of their duffel bags onto flatbeds. I had to find a SGM (Sergeant Major who is the highest enlisted ranking other than a CSM Command Sergeant Major) to have him locate my duffel bags, because I was returning to Arizona, not Germany.

Just before talking to the Sergeant Major, I met two other soldiers who were in the same dilemma. One had received a Red Cross emergency message and one was a Reservist. They both were stationed in the States, and not in Germany, so they needed their duffel bags downloaded too. Fortunately, the SGM was kind enough to have his soldiers download the duffel bags so we could locate ours.

When I stood in line at the ticket counter to get my airline tickets to return to the states, it was brought to my attention that my orders stated my return was only to Germany. I was to return with 1AD to Germany because that's where they were stationed, not in the States. So, I had to find my original orders that sent me to Saudi from the states. That meant I had to get into my duffel bag and go through everything.

People were everywhere in the military airport at Rhein Mein. There were a lot of duffel bags piled up in areas and a couple of soldiers came up and asked me, "Red Cross, would you mind watching our duffel bags for a couple of hours while we go out and see what there is around here?"

I said, "No problem, just leave them there." After finding my original orders, I stood back in line at the ticket counter and finally got the same agent. I was then told that I would have to return on "seats available" and the only ones currently available were for those with emergency leave. She didn't know how long I would have to wait.

I went back to the duffel bags and sprawled out of top of them and decided to try to take a nap. After an hour or so, the soldiers returned whom I was "duffel bag sitting for" and they collected their bags. I then met four soldiers who were on emergency leave waiting to get on the next available flight out. One guy said, "thanks" to me for helping him regarding his emergency leave. He said he was going out on a small plane that was carrying a dead body back to the states from the war. It was kind of an eerie feeling, but he didn't care. He just needed to get out of there.

"Well thank you, but I'm probably not the one who worked your case", I said.

"I don't care . . . it feels good to say thanks to a Red Cross person." I smiled and advised him that he didn't have to wait on a military plane to return home. All he had to do was go to the Red Cross there at the airport and I was sure they would give him assistance.

Fortunately his flight came through and he left 1 ½ hrs. later on a military plane. The Reservist whom I met earlier was Sgt. Ellenheiser. He walked up to me to see when I was leaving because he had just been told that there was a new flight scheduled to go out at 2115 hrs that night arriving in Philadelphia and he was booked on it. I went back to the ticketing agent and a lady said, "Yes, so far they had six available seats.

I quickly told her that I wanted to be assigned to one and she said, "Okay".

2115 hrs came and went and we kept checking and finally at 0315 hrs the next morning, 2 May we were informed that all flights had been canceled.

Sgt. Ellenheiser informed me that there was a "Tent city" located outside Rhein Mein airfield but we would have a long walk to get to it. He had been to Germany before as a Reservist and knew it was close by, close enough to walk to.

That was fine with me.

We locked our bags in the lockers at the airport and got out into the cold air and found "Tent City". He went to the men's area and I went to the ladies sleeping area. At 0700 hrs we met for breakfast and he showed me where the mess hall was that we were going to eat at.

We then returned to Rhein Mein airport and were told that there was a 72-hr hold on all flights leaving. Sgt. Ellenheiser told me he was going to catch a taxi to the main international airport and charge a return ticket on his charge card. I called my Supervisor at Western Operations Headquarters and informed her that I, too, was going to charge a ticket and not hang around the military airport any longer. I felt I had been patient long enough. They understood.

Sgt. Ellenheiser and I both called the International Airlines and booked us flights out of there. We then went back to get our duffel bags out of the lockers, but I couldn't find my key. I couldn't believe it. I had to pay for someone to come and break the lock. I have no idea what happened to that darn key. I felt like a fool, but I was still happy because I knew I was going home soon. In fact, I was actually flying that afternoon.

May 2, 1440 hrs I was on my way home. There was a connecting flight I had to take when we landed in Atlanta, Georgia. Sgt. Ellenheiser and I split directions and then I boarded my final flight home. The stewardess gave me a bottle of champagne and upon my arrival on May 3, in Tucson; my family and friends, including my new friend George, greeted me. It was wonderful being back home and seeing everyone I had missed so much. I knew that I needed some time to regroup and take a long, hot bath.

I hadn't realized it, but I had lost 18 pounds. I now weighed 100 lbs. and looked horrible. When I tried to eat, it gave me diarrhea and I couldn't eat much. My stomach had shrunk, probably because I only ate 1/3 of each MRE package for each meal.

I had a beautiful tan, but later found out it was the stain from the sand and dirt that eventually washed off.

My first meal consisted of a beer and pizza. I ate one slice of pizza and ¼ glass of beer. It was very filling. I didn't realize how tired I really was. Once I was able to relax and wind down, it was like a bomb hit me and I lost a lot of energy. It took me a while to get my energy level back to its normal peak. I also found that it was difficult to sleep. If you weren't dreaming of the scud attacks, then you were missing the noise from the generators that you were accustomed to hearing all the time.

There was a Welcome Home Parade of which I got to participate in and the Vietnam vets made sure our returning people knew they were appreciated and not forgotten.

George and I got together two or three times after that. He was ready to find someone who was willing to provide him with children, where I on the other hand, wasn't about to consider starting another family.

He separated from the Air Force and went on to fly planes.

I eventually went back to work where I transferred within the County and became the Reenactment Director for 88-Crime, for Pima County Attorneys' office.

I later decided that my heart was still with the American Red Cross, so I went to work full time for them, and moved to Niceville, FL assigned to Eglin Air Force Base.

I had a big surprise before I departed for Florida. Captain Bellows (remember the one who was cussing up a storm?) paid me a surprise visit. He was stationed in Texas, and decided to take a few days off and see Arizona. We saw each other a couple of more times until I was sent to Germany one year later as the Station Manager in Kaiserslautern, Germany. He went on with his Army missions, and I went on with my life. We made a vow that even though we may never see each other again; we were going to be friends forever. A permanent bond, which would never be broken.

After being stationed in Germany for over two years, I met a wonderful man, who is now my husband.

I then graduated with a Bachelor's Degree from Wayland Baptist University with high honors.

This book is not sponsored, endorsed, or authorized by the American Red Cross.

WORDS OF ADVICE TO THOSE RETURNING AND TO FAMILY MEMBERS AND FRIENDS

There are several things I'd like to emphasize regarding the returning of people who've been deployed. Even though psychologically they think they are ready to resume normal duties at home upon their return, reality shows that bodies are not quite up to it. People normally want to make up for the time they've lost, and sometimes families are disappointed to see that they're not as active as they had hoped. All of this will take time, and no one can "make up for lost time". You can love though, and love each other every time you're together.

Patience is the name of the game on both sides. Everyone is eager to see the other member, and the need to "take charge" again upon one's return will need to be slowly resumed. Those deployed need to remember someone else has been in charge since they've been gone, and it will now have to be discussed and slowly taken over, if at all.

Just because people in the same unit may have experienced the same thing in their deployment, it does not mean that they have been able to tolerate it the same. Every person is a unique individual and may look, respond, or accept things completely differently than someone else.

Many have had to deal with things like killing, death, the smell of death, the loss of a fellow soldier, etc., and they don't expect you to understand . . . just be a little tolerable. Just listen.

Some may not want to talk about things, but are free to talk to their comrades because they know they will understand. . . . because they were there. Do not take it personal. If they choose to talk to family members, then listen and don't find fault. Share in their experiences if they're willing to discuss it

There is plenty of counseling available and it is always best to work through any issues you may have. Family Assistance is on every military base or post, and if you'd prefer, go to a counselor in the city. Some may not need counseling because they've been able to have open communication and have learned how to talk lovingly to each other.

Both need to remember not to criticize the other and if there's a major problem, seek help. Remember, it takes two people to make any relationship work.

One of the most important things to remember and never forget is our Missing in Action from Desert Storm and all conflicts. According to a site on the Internet under "Desert Storm", the last known count was 38. One is too many. We have so many from previous wars, and we must keep pushing for answers and never forget!

POWs and MIAs, you will not be forgotten!